the case for law school

VICTORIA NICHOLLS
WITH
CHRISTOPHER C. NICHOLLS

UNIVERSITY OF TORONTO PRESS
Toronto Buffalo London

The Case for Law School

Irwin Law
An imprint of University of Toronto Press
Toronto Buffalo London
utppublishing.com
Printed in Canada

ISBN 978-1-4875-7136-8 (paper) | ISBN 978-1-4875-7138-2 (EPUB)
ISBN 978-1-4875-7137-5 (PDF)

Library and Archives Canada Cataloguing in Publication

Title: The case for law school / Victoria Nicholls with Christopher C. Nicholls.
Names: Nicholls, Victoria, author. | Nicholls, Christopher C., author
Description: Includes bibliographical references and index.
Identifiers: Canadiana (print) 20250247658 | Canadiana (ebook) 20250247682 | ISBN 9781487571368 (paper) | ISBN 9781487571375 (PDF) | ISBN 9781487571382 (EPUB)
Subjects: LCSH: Law schools – Canada – Admission.
Classification: LCC KE309 .N53 2025 | LCC KF275 .N53 2025 kfmod | DDC 340.071/171–dc23

Cover design: Alan Jones
Cover image: Brian A Jackson/Shutterstock.com

We wish to acknowledge the land on which the University of Toronto Press operates. This land is the traditional territory of the Wendat, the Anishnaabeg, the Haudenosaunee, the Métis, and the Mississaugas of the Credit First Nation.

University of Toronto Press acknowledges the financial support of the Government of Canada, the Canada Council for the Arts, and the Ontario Arts Council, an agency of the Government of Ontario, for its publishing activities.

Canada Council for the Arts
Conseil des Arts du Canada

ONTARIO ARTS COUNCIL
CONSEIL DES ARTS DE L'ONTARIO
an Ontario government agency
un organisme du gouvernement de l'Ontario

Funded by the Government of Canada
Financé par le gouvernement du Canada
Canada

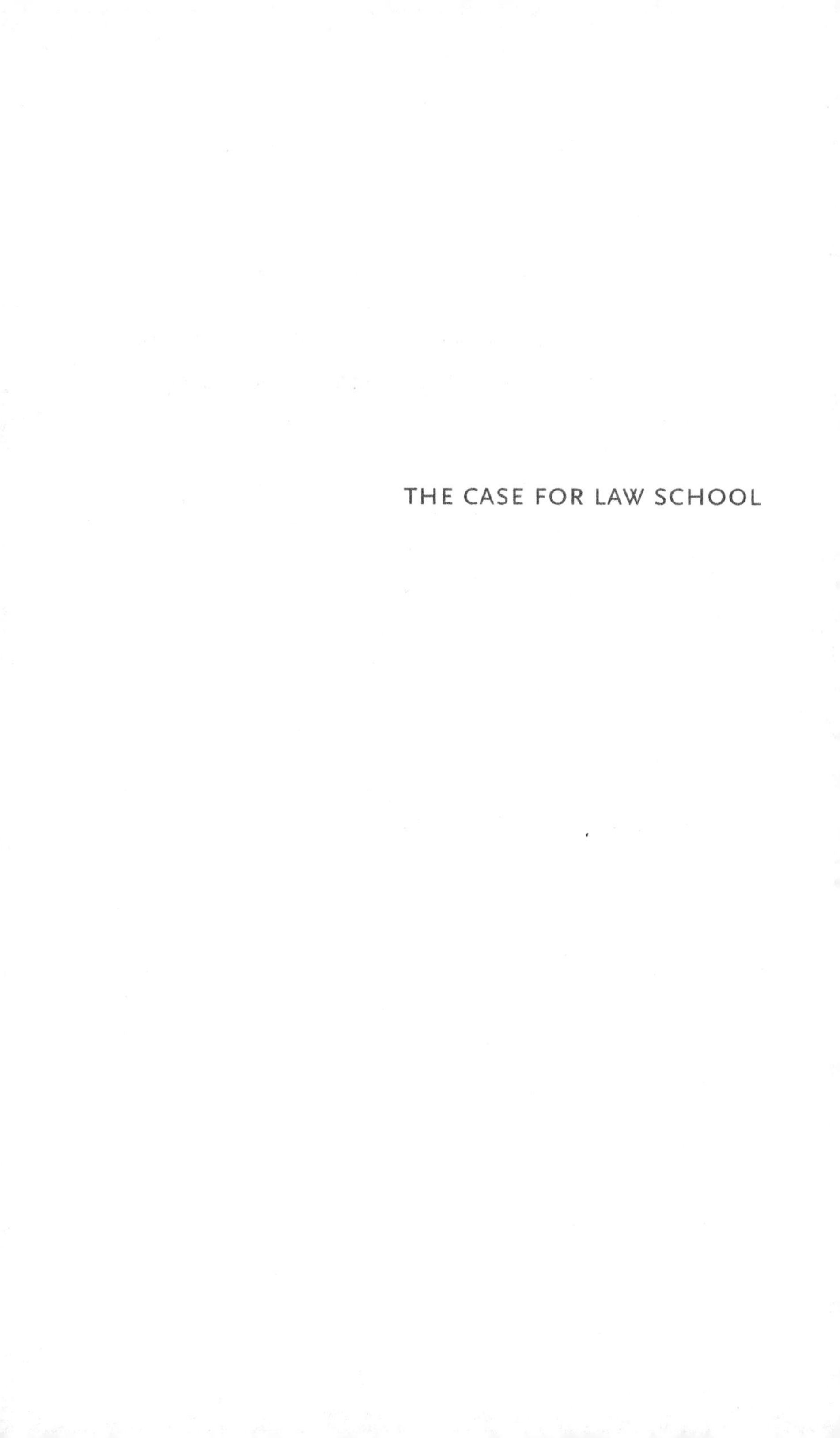

THE CASE FOR LAW SCHOOL

PREVIOUS IRWIN LAW BOOKS
BY CHRISTOPHER NICHOLLS

Securities Law, Third Edition (2023)

Mergers, Acquisitions and Other Changes of Corporate Control, Third Edition (2020)

summary

TABLE OF CONTENTS

detailed

TABLE OF CONTENTS

preface

This book represents an unusual collaboration between father and daughter: one (CN), an experienced law professor, the other (TN), a recent university graduate.

We hope the readers of this book – university students and others interested in the subject of law schools and legal education – will find this a refreshing collaboration.

When she was a residence don at the University of Toronto, TN saw first-hand the stress, anxiety, and uncertainty facing many students nearing graduation as they considered their next steps. One of the most popular options for those graduates was law school. But unless students had family members or friends within the legal profession, it was frustratingly hard to get a clear picture about what to expect in law school. And since the cost of applying to law school is high – and the cost of actually attending many times higher – she thought there was a need for a book exploring some of the ins and outs of getting in and getting the most out of law school, written from the perspective of someone who was herself considering law as a possible career option.

In the meantime, CN, like most Canadian law school professors, had been reflecting on and re-evaluating the changing role of Canadian law school education. Age-old debates over how law schools should balance theory and practice have been reinvigorated with particular urgency in the twenty-first century and interwoven with challenges for law schools to wrestle with broader questions of the role of law and lawyers in building a more just society. Catalysts for law school renewal and reform include, among many others, the release of the Carnegie Foundation's 2007 report, *Educating Lawyers: Preparation for the Profession of Law,* along with a series of historic developments in Canadian legal education, including the founding of several new law schools, the Federation of Law Societies of Canada's National Requirement, and the Truth and Reconciliation Committee's Calls to Action.

Canadian law schools are changing. And so, we have worked together to create what we hope will be a useful, at times thought-provoking (or perhaps just provoking), law school resource.

We have tried to offer information, insight, and occasionally advice on topics ranging from applying to law school to getting the most out of law school classes and exams, and even to figuring out how to become qualified to practise law after graduation.

Our goal is not to convince you to attend law school, but to help you understand law school a little better so you can decide if it might be a good fit for you.

While writing this book, CN was a visiting scholar at Stanford Law School and a senior visiting academic at Oxford University's Faculty of Law Commercial Law Centre. He wishes to thank Michael Klausner at Stanford Law School and Kristin van Zwieten, the director of the Commercial Law Centre at Harris Manchester College, Oxford, as well as John Armour, Dean of the Oxford Faculty of Law, for their help and support during these wonderful academic visits. He also acknowledges and thanks his colleagues at Western University Faculty of Law. Above all, as always, he offers his warmest thanks and gratitude to his wife, Andrea, whose contribution to every project is invaluable and who was uniquely essential to this book as the mother of his co-author.

TN wants to thank the many students at Victoria College, U of T, for the conversations that inspired her to try to put this book project together, as well as to her Mom, who patiently put up with the endless conversations between her and her co-author over the phone, Zoom, and occasionally the dinner table talking about Christopher Columbus Langdell and Harvard Law School in the nineteenth century, why law schools still attach so much importance to the LSAT, and whether an auction bid to buy something called a "worm-tub" is, or is not, a contract.

TN
Toronto, Ontario
February 2025

CN
London, Ontario
February 2025

part one
introduction

1

opening statement

As Jane Austen might have said (if Jane Austen were a twenty-first-century university student), "it is a truth universally acknowledged that a young person who has recently completed a BA must be in search of a law degree."

Law is seen as a secure profession. A lucrative profession. A profession that is sure to make your parents proud and your "frenemies" (if you grew up in the 1990s) envious.

Picture this: It's a hot afternoon in late May or June. Convocation Day. You have just graduated with your English degree (or your degree in philosophy/history/fine arts/communications/criminology/sociology/postmodern acupuncture and furniture design, or what have you). You proudly walk across the stage in your mortar-board cap and rented graduation gown ready to shake the hand of the chancellor of the university, who is sweating profusely under academic robes as colourful as a circus costume.

"You did it!" you think to yourself. "This is what all that hard work and those thousands of dollars in student debt have all led up to." And as you stand on that stage, smiling for the photographer (to whom you will soon be paying a few more hundred dollars for a set of beautifully air-brushed prints in more assorted sizes than you have distant relatives to send them to), you pretend not to see your parents, who are aggressively waving at you from their seats, as you think, "Now what?"

You have received a wonderful education . . . or so every 50-year-old keeps reminding you. You know the difference between a Shakespearean and a Petrarchan sonnet. You not only understand the finer points of the Treaty of Versailles, you also have been known to occasionally bring the subject up at parties, despite the obvious lack of any interest in the room. You have firmly decided that you ethically disagree with the concept of psychological egoism (because if you *do* agree with psychological egoism – the notion that human beings act only in ways that benefit themselves – why would anyone watch televised golf?). And, of course, you are now the proud owner of a beautifully calligraphed diploma adorned with your university's ornate embossed seal and an inspiring Latin motto (that most graduates can't actually read). But that's about all you are sure of.

Still, you've always been told you're "good at arguing" and that "you have a talent for public speaking." And I'm sure at least once during the four years you spent sitting in university lecture halls and library carrels, some well-meaning professor, classmate, or kindly family member has posed the inevitable question, "Have you thought about law school?"

So, have you?

Really?

Lucky for you, I have, too. And I want to share with you what I've found. Hopefully, this information about law and law school will be useful to you. I have taken considerable time and great care looking into this. It became a bit of a personal mission for me. When I first finished university, I decided to get a job rather than go right back to school. It was a pretty good job, and I worked very hard. I learned a lot about business and found it surprisingly interesting. My income jumped up fairly quickly. Things seemed to be going well. But I still couldn't help wondering about law school. Would it be right for me? Would it be worth it? Frankly, I wasn't sure; so I knew I needed to gather as much information as I could find. I went to work on learning more.

And for all the information I couldn't source on my own, I've turned to my Dad to help me out. Who is my Dad, you ask? He is none other than Ryan Reynolds himself.

I'm kidding, obviously. He's actually a law professor . . . so the opposite of Ryan Reynolds, basically. Now, he may not know much about running Welsh soccer teams, but he is pretty helpful when it comes to getting an accurate idea of what law school is like and, you know, whether someone might actually want to study law and eventually become a lawyer. After spending many long hours (in several different countries) investigating law school on my own and "fact checking" some of my research with him, it seemed to both of us that other prospective law students might also be interested in what we've learned. That's why we decided to write this book.

So let's dive in. What is the case for going (or not going) to law school? We will try to lay out the evidence for you. When you have finished this book, I hope you will have a much better idea about what law school is really about and whether you actually want to apply to law school.

And, hopefully, so will I.

part two
applying to law school

2

to apply or not to apply? that is the ($315+) question

Introduction

Remember in high school when your favourite teacher told you, "to succeed, you are going to have to apply yourself"? Well, that's certainly true for law school. To attend, you are going to have to apply. Yourself. In this chapter, I plan to walk you through many of the specifics about the law school application process. The goal is to give you a good idea of what to expect if you decide to apply. It won't be easy. It is not an inexpensive process, and it is very time consuming. (The law school applications, I mean. Not writing this chapter.) I'll explain the OLSAS (Ontario Law School Application Service) and the LSAT (Law School Admission Test) as well as all the information you may or may not have wanted to know but will probably need. Will any of this be entertaining? Only you can be the judge of that. Will you still want to apply when you see what is in store for you? Who's to say?

Can You Pay the Price?

> *The best things in life are free.*
> *But they won't get you a law degree.*

Perhaps the first question you need to ask yourself is this: "Do you have what it takes to apply to law school?" What it takes to apply to law school is $315.[1] (At least.)

Obviously, law school is a long-term investment. The out-of-pocket cost should not be the most important consideration. But it isn't trivial, either. There's no point throwing hard-earned money away before you have taken steps to prepare yourself for the demanding and at times unusual law school application process.

Can You Emotionally Afford to Apply?

I am not joking about the emotional cost. It is real, it is significant, and it should not be overlooked. This won't come as a shock to anyone. Law school applications are long and gruelling. They can take hours, weeks, or even months to complete. It is no easy feat to balance the pressures of university or full-time work with the time and energy demanded in completing multiple law school applications. Unfortunately, the only way to get into law school is to apply. (I'll let you know if I

1 This is the cost of applying to a single Ontario law school through the OLSAS portal in 2024. OLSAS charges $200, and the cost of applying to each school is an additional $115. These charges do not include the other fees that go into applying to law school, such as the cost for taking the LSAT or any application fees payable if you were to apply to a school outside of Ontario.

figure out another way. That's what second editions are for.) So the first thing to keep in mind when you are considering applying is that you will need to make sure you can set aside enough time for the application process.

Given the time, financial, and emotional burdens of applying, it is important to be sure you have a good idea about what exactly you are applying for. Are you sure law school is for you? What should you expect from law school if you are admitted? Is it worth it? To try to answer these questions, we will need to dive a little more deeply into what to expect at law school. We will begin to look more closely at that beginning in chapter 4.

Do You Really Want to Go to Law School, or Have You Just Watched Too Much TV?

Trust me. We've all been there. Anyone who tells you any differently is lying. And by "there" I mean we've just finished sitting through an old episode of *Suits*. Or we've scrolled on Instagram where we've watched three different reels featuring lawyers explaining exactly why Amber Heard lost that lawsuit against Johnny Depp. We watched. We listened. We dreamed. And we thought, "Man, I want to do that job."

I'm right there with you. The lure of the law is unmistakable. But there's also something undeniably appealing about the prestige of law school itself. I won't pretend that I wasn't at least slightly enticed to consider applying to law school by a certain cheeky line from the 2001 film *Legally Blonde*. When asked by her astonished ex-boyfriend how she ever managed to get into Harvard Law School, an unfazed Elle Woods (hilariously portrayed by Reese Witherspoon) breezily replies, "What? Like it's hard?"[2]

Of course, getting into any law school in real life *is* hard. And expensive. And time consuming. If becoming a successful lawyer was just about being able to wear expensive clothes or bringing Amber Heard to tears on the witness stand, that might not be (quite) enough. But there are also many other serious reasons to think about going to law school and becoming a lawyer.

From the time most of us were children we have all had a sense that some things are simply unfair, that power can be abused, and that many people need and deserve help to protect their dignity and their basic rights. As we get older, we develop new ways of thinking about those fundamental ideas and the timeless concept that lies behind them all: justice.

What is justice? That's a big question. Plato's *Republic* is basically one long attempt at answering that question (a really long attempted answer, as you probably know if you have been lucky enough to have read it). Philosophers, political scientists, economists, and even psychologists all have insights to offer on what justice means and how it might be achieved. But law school, at least when you're peeking over the fence

2 One thing has always bothered me about some people's reaction to Elle Woods's apparently effortless admission to Harvard Law School and her precocious courtroom prowess in *Legally Blonde*. The audience is told she scored a 179 on the LSAT. That is just one mark short of a perfect 180 and would place Elle in the top .02 percent of all test takers. As we explain in chapter 3, the creators of the LSAT claim it is an aptitude test. Elle Woods is basically a genius. So Elle wasn't a struggling underdog whose hard work ultimately paid off. It was just that most people watching the film overlooked that she was always a straight-up genius because she happened to be blonde and appreciated fashion. OK. Sorry. Just had to get that off my chest.

from the outside, seems to be a uniquely appropriate place to learn more about what justice is while you actually prepare to work one day at a job where you can apply that knowledge in practice.

At least that's the theory. But even though justice is important to everyone, that doesn't necessarily mean that "lawyering" is the right kind of job or that law school is the right kind of education for everyone. So now is the time to think about whether this is something you *really* want to do and is likely to be a good fit for your talents, interests, and aspirations.

Canadian Law Schools

Let's start with the basics. There are law schools all across Canada. Everyone knows that just because you want to be a lawyer in, say, Alberta, doesn't mean you have to go to law school in Alberta. You have choices. So how does that work? Law schools in Canada are all the same, right? Wrong. There are some important basic facts about the structure of Canadian common law schools that are important to keep in mind before you start filling in those multi-page application forms. And now we will begin to see why having a law professor as a father comes in handy. I was bound to find a reason eventually. (I kid.)

A Fireside Chat (Sort of)

Imagine you're watching a "fireside chat." I, Tori Nicholls (TN), am sitting on a large tufted-back leather chair on one side of the fire (enchanting, isn't it?), taking notes on a clipboard. On the other side of the fireside sits my father, Christopher Nicholls (CN), the law professor.

Note: The dialogue between TN (Victoria "Tori" Nicholls) and CN (Christopher Nicholls) extends throughout the book.

TN: I know that going to law school, on its own, does not give you the right to start practising law in Canada. You also have to complete bar admission examinations and satisfy an "experiential" training component either through a kind of legal internship or apprenticeship called "articling" or by completing a special Law Practice Program. (We'll deal with those things in more detail in chapter 10.) But law school is the important first step. How many law schools can a person apply to in Canada?

CN: That depends. Canada's legal system has sometimes been described as "bijural" because it is based on two different traditional systems: the English common law system and the French civil law system. More recently, a growing recognition of, and deep respect for, Indigenous law and legal orders means that the term "multijural" or "polyjural" might more fully describe the legal system. There are also, broadly speaking, two main types of law school programs in Canada: common law programs and civil law programs, as well as an integrated common law/civil law degree program (leading to degrees in both civil law and common law) offered by the Faculty of Law at McGill University and a four-year joint degree program in common law and Indigenous legal orders offered by the University of Victoria Faculty of Law, alongside its three-year common law degree program. If your goal is to practise law in Quebec, the only jurisdiction in Canada with a Civil Code that traces its roots to the French Napoleonic Code, then you will need to attend a school that grants a civil law degree. Most (though not all) of the civil law schools in Canada are in Quebec. They are very fine schools, but this book is really about Canada's common law schools; so we won't say any more about the civil law schools here.

Canadian common law schools are approved or accredited by the governing bodies of the legal profession in each province. The legal profession in each province is regulated by its own provincial law society. These provincial law societies operate under provincial legislation. They control entry into the profession and administer the discipline process for practising lawyers in their respective provinces.

TN: And the provincial law societies also decide which law schools qualify a person to become eligible to become a lawyer in that province?

CN: Yes. And, although the law profession is regulated province-by-province, the provincial law societies also work together on a national level through the Federation of Law Societies of Canada (FLSC). The FLSC accredits (or approves) Canadian common law school programs. That means that any person who graduates from any approved common law school in Canada – regardless of which province the law school is located in – is eligible to be admitted to the bar admission program in any Canadian common law province.

This national accreditation system also has implications for the curricula at Canadian common law schools. The FLSC has promulgated a "National Requirement," which is a document that sets out the knowledge and skills that graduates of approved common law schools are expected to have.[3] This National Requirement is reviewed every five years. A new version of the National Requirement was approved in 2024 and is expected to take effect in 2029. That means that it will apply to graduates of Canadian common law schools beginning in the spring of 2029; so this will be the version of the National Requirement that will apply to most readers of this book who are applying to enter law school from the fall of 2026 going forward.

TN: Does that mean that the programs at all Canadian law schools – at least the common law programs – will all be basically the same?

CN: The National Requirement is a fairly high-level document. It gives the law schools plenty of room to decide for themselves how best to satisfy the requirements. But it does include a number of specific matters, too. There are also two common law schools that offer an integrated practice curriculum, which incorporates the sort of hands-on practical experience that graduates from most other law schools aren't really exposed to until they begin their articles of clerkship – that "experiential" requirement you referred to. (We will say more about this in chapter 10.)

However, apart from these exceptions, though there are certainly differences, I think it may fairly be said that the basic programs at Canadian common law schools are all substantially similar in most material respects.

---

3 Federation of Law Societies of Canada, *National Requirement* (in effect January 1, 2029), online (pdf): https://flsc.ca/wp-content/uploads/2024/04/NRR-approved-on-March-12-2024-ENG.pdf.

TN: So for anyone hoping to practise law in any common law province, attending any one of the common law school programs will make them eligible to be admitted to their own province's bar admission program. Now, I've learned that there are 19 common law school programs in Canada.[4] *Of those 19 common law schools, 18 are schools that offer instruction in English.*[5] *So those are the schools that those of us in common law provinces who are only considering English-language programs have to choose from. The law degree offered by each of these schools is a JD (juris doctor).*

CN: We will have more to say later on about why law degrees at Canadian common law schools are today called "JDs." For now, I would only point out that, even though the "D" stands for "doctor," the JD degree is not considered a "doctoral" degree.

---

4 Technically, there are 21. But there are only 19 schools that offer a traditional three-year JD degree. The Université de Montréal (UdeM) offers a special JD degree (in addition to their distinguished three-year civil law degree program). UdeM's one-year French-language JD is offered as a graduate degree program to which only holders of an undergraduate degree in (civil) law may be admitted. There are additional conditions applicants must satisfy to be eligible to apply for this program. The Université de Sherbrooke also offers a special one-year JD degree. For a complete list of approved common law JD programs in Canada, see Federation of Law Societies of Canada, "Approved Canadian Common Law School Programs," online (pdf): https://flsc.ca/wp-content/uploads/2023/11/Schools-EN-V8.pdf.

5 Most of these schools only offer three-year JD (common law) programs in English. But there are three exceptions. McGill University's Faculty of Law offers a bilingual "transsystemic" law program in which graduating students obtain both a JD (common law) degree and a Bachelor of Civil Law. The University of Ottawa is also unique among Canadian law schools because it has both an English common law program and a French common law program as well as an intensive eight-month JD program for candidates who already possess a civil law degree. The University of Ottawa also has a civil law degree program. Finally, the University of Victoria offers not only a traditional three-year common law JD degree but also a four-year joint JD/JID degree program in Canadian common law and Indigenous legal orders.

TN: So if I were to graduate from law school, would I get to call myself "Doctor"?

CN: No.

TN: Well, we will see . . . (I mean, for example, suppose you were speaking to someone who hadn't read this book. Who would really know? Just saying.)

CN: No. You can't do that.

TN: So, it sounds like it might still be sort of an open question.

CN: No. It isn't.

TN: I'm sure there are competing views about this.

CN: No. There really aren't.[6]

The Common Law Schools

So maybe you won't be able to call yourself "Doctor" (although could there be a freedom of speech issue, here? Just putting it out there). But you will be looking into how to earn a "JD" degree. One of the 19 Canadian common law schools, the Université de Moncton, offers a JD common law degree entirely in the French language. In this book, however, we are going to focus on the 18 English-speaking common law schools in Canada. Now, of those 18 schools, 8 are in Ontario. About 3,030 first-year students are admitted into JD programs across Canada each year. Of those 3,030 first-year places, more than 1,600 of them are at Ontario schools.

6 Intriguingly, however, there has been a lively discussion of this issue in the United States, leading to various differing ethical pronouncements. See David Perry, "How Did Lawyers Become Doctors" (2012) 84:5 NY St PAJ 20 at 23.

Here is why that might matter. On some online law school discussion forums, you will often see people repeat the advice that, all else being equal, it makes most sense to go to law school in the same jurisdiction in which you eventually intend to practise law. Of course, there might be some good practical advantages to following this advice. For example, perhaps you might have a better chance at making contacts with lawyers in local firms. That might help in your eventual job search. Maybe some of your courses will tend to emphasize unique features of your home province's legislation that are important in specific areas of legal practice. But because a JD degree from any Canadian common law school is recognized in every Canadian common law province, it might also make sense to at least think about applying to schools in Ontario (as well as your home province) no matter where you expect to work in the future. Apart from anything else, there is a disproportionate number of spaces in Ontario law schools.

What Does It Take to Get In?

We all know that, whatever Elle Woods may have thought, it's not easy to get into law school. Let's start with each university's publicly posted statistics. But first, a word of caution. While I think it's important to be aware of these statistics before applying, they don't tell the whole story. I want to emphasize that these statistics should by no means intimidate or deter you from applying if you really want to go to law school. The first thing to remember is that the numbers provided for each university are averages, or what the university calls a "competitive GPA/LSAT score." That necessarily means some people who were admitted – perhaps as many as half the class – had lower statistics. And the pool of applicants every year will be different. According to the Law School Admissions Council (LSAC), there have been various ranges in applicants and application numbers from year to year. For example, there were 8,150 applicants to Canadian law school programs in 2021 but only 7,351 in 2022.[7] Who's to say whether it would have been any easier to get in in 2022, but it was at least the case that applicants that year were competing against a smaller pool. That means that the particular year you happen to apply can really affect the likelihood of whether you get accepted or not. Is that fair? Probably not. Is that life? Unfortunately.

In Appendix A at the end of this chapter, we have included a chart with summary application information from the 18 English-language common law school programs in Canada. The chart lists the law schools in alphabetical order and shows you for the most recent year at the time of writing, on average, how many applications each school received, how many spots were available in their first-year class, the average GPA score for accepted applicants, and the average LSAT score for accepted applicants. The information on this chart only includes statistics for applicants in the "General" applicant category for each law school. Law schools also have a number of special application categories that are based on a wider range of personal characteristics and experiences. GPA and LSAT scores do not feature as prominently in the assessment of applications in these special categories.

---

7 LSAC, "YTD Canadian Applicants from Region/Province of Permanent Residence," online: https://report.lsac.org/VolumeSummary.aspx.

Because the applicant pool differs every year, this chart is really only intended to give you a general idea of approximately what LSAT scores and university grades you may need to make you a competitive candidate at each school. These numbers should not be taken as official statistics. As the appendix explains, some have been drawn from information published by the schools themselves. But in some cases, I have relied on information from third-party sources. What this chart cannot tell you, of course, is how your entire application – including the unique combination of your grades, test scores, experiences, and accomplishments – compares to the material submitted by your fellow applicants. It is therefore impossible to determine, based on this sort of historical statistical information, whether you will or will not get into any particular law school.

What Are Law Schools Looking For?

TN: Admission statistics are an important source of information for prospective students. But they don't seem to tell the whole story. Law school applicants spend a lot of time speculating about their chances of admission. Online law school forums, for example, are filled with anxious applicants' "chances" threads. What else are law schools looking for besides high grade point averages and LSAT scores?

CN: Law schools are all looking for bright, motivated, thoughtful, intellectually curious and mature students with diverse backgrounds and perspectives. Admissions officers and admissions committees know that every applicant is unique and that undergraduate grade point averages and LSAT scores can never begin to provide anything like an accurate picture of a person's talents. Many schools ask for reference letters to help them get a broader perspective on applicants, and most schools invite applicants to write personal essays or statements in which they can help the admissions office get a better understanding of their personality, their values, any exceptional challenges they have had to overcome, and other unique ways they will be able to contribute to the incoming class and, eventually, to the legal community and broader society.

TN: When I hear this I think that it might be possible for my personal essay to somehow rescue my whole application. Is that the case?

CN: All of the information in your application is important and is considered carefully. But applicants must also appreciate that university grades and LSAT scores necessarily play a very important role in the application process for at least two reasons. First, law is a very demanding academic program. Undergraduate grades and LSAT scores – considered together – are important indicators of an applicant's future academic success at law school. Second, grades and especially LSAT scores provide directly comparable information, although one is always sensitive to the difficulty of comparing grade point averages from different institutions and different undergraduate degree programs.

TN: So does that mean that I'm set up to do well in law school if I come in with high marks and a high LSAT? And if I have low scores, is it simply a waste of time (and money) to apply?

CN: Grades and test scores are certainly not perfect predictors. Everyone understands that. Many people admitted to law school with high GPAs and high LSATs may discover that law school isn't a good fit for them, while some people with lower GPAs and lower LSATs thrive at law school and go on to succeed brilliantly at the practice of law too, for that matter.

TN: So if you're saying that they are not necessarily a reliable indicator of law school performance and that you have had successful law school students with lower GPA and LSAT scores, why the heck are we still using this process to assess law school applications?

CN: Because despite their well-known limitations, undergraduate grades and LSAT scores are still, on average, a reasonable (if imperfect) predictor of law school performance (at least in the first year). Because of the very large number of applications every Canadian law school receives, university grades and LSAT scores are one important way of helping to initially evaluate applicants in the general admission category.

TN: But test scores and grades are less determinative for students who are applying in special access categories?

CN: Yes. The very point of special access categories of admission is to fairly recognize that some students have acquired significant work or life experience, or have overcome significant hurdles or disadvantages that also indicate abilities that will help them succeed in law school. They may also bring unique perspectives that will illuminate their approach to the study and practice of law in ways that offer important benefits to the law school community and the broader community following graduation.

TN: But for most applicants it sounds like a high LSAT and GPA score will be critical to getting into law school. So does that mean if I have average grades and a so-so LSAT I should give up, even though I'm certain I want to go to law school?

CN: Not necessarily. Some applicants have extraordinary personal accomplishments that can compensate for – or explain – somewhat weaker university grades or LSAT scores. In those cases, it may well be worth applying to highly competitive law schools, always recognizing that one must be realistic about the likelihood of admission.

TN: I think everyone understands that important parts of a law school application are strictly a matter of numbers: GPAs and LSAT scores. But what about the other parts of the application that deal with all those other "soft" skills and unique personal experiences, characteristics, and perspectives you mentioned? How do you make those parts of your application to law school stand out from the crowd?

CN: Let me offer one important caveat: Although professors are often members of admission committees (and I have served on admission committees in the past), every law school has experienced full-time professionals in their admissions offices whose views on these issues may well differ from mine. Now, before we can tackle your question, it may be useful to step back and ask what sort of applications do *not* really stand out from the crowd and, in the process, offer some thoughts about what, exactly, one is applying to. Tolstoy once wrote, "All happy families resemble one another; every unhappy family is unhappy in its own way."[8] In the case of law school applications, the

8 Leo Tolstoy, *Anna Karenina* ("Все счастливые семьи похожи друг на друга, каждая несчастливая семья несчастлива по- своему").

reverse is often true: Each outstanding application is outstanding in its own way; weaker applications tend to look a lot alike.

TN: *Not to mention that, these days, applications written by AI software apps like ChatGPT all have irritating similarities, catch phrases, and formatting formulas. These are dead giveaways, even when people have provided specific information about themselves to try to customize their responses. Once, when reviewing job applications in a previous position I held, I saw the phrase "tangible experience" and "live events" in a dozen different applications. Even if you could define "tangible experience" no one but an LLM algorithm would use such a phrase. Tossing away those resumes was a very rewarding "tangible experience" for me. But it sounds like you may have something more specific in mind. Are the weaknesses that you are talking about shortcomings in things like extracurricular activities, or do they have more to do with the tone or style of the application?*

CN: I was thinking, first, about some of the overworn clichés that appear in many applications. For example, there are two especially common themes found in many lacklustre law school application personal statements. The first is some version of, "I want to give back." Now, it is natural enough for applicants to think admissions officers will be pleased (or even relieved) to hear that they are guided by an admirable sense of social consciousness. The problem is, when you see similar language time and time again from so many applicants it begins to seem artificial. The important thing is not simply to make vague and unsubstantiated claims about your commitment to do good works, but to provide persuasive evidence of that commitment.

TN: OK, but what if I do really want to give back? I think many people that I know are very sincere about their commitment to their communities. They aren't just saying what they think the law schools want to hear. How do we let the admissions office know that? It seems a little unfair and cynical to me that someone reading an application would be skeptical about personal statements. (I am saying "we" here, although personally I just want to sell my soul to the corporate law world and keep everything for myself. Obviously I'm kidding. Obviously.)

CN: Please don't misunderstand. Of course, it's a very positive, very human, and highly worthwhile thing to want to live a life of real purpose and be a force for good in your community. The difficulty is that it is very easy for anyone – including your hypothetical "soul seller" – to talk about how selfless they are. Unless there is concrete evidence elsewhere in the application of a genuine *serious* commitment to something other than opportunistic résumé building, statements of this sort tend to ring rather hollow (at least to me). That's a problem because unsupported statements like this may sometimes have the paradoxical effect of making an applicant actually seem more self-centred and even disingenuous.

TN: Ok. So it is probably best to avoid vague cookie-cutter statements about "giving back to the community" or "making a difference" or "protecting the environment" or "planning to use my law degree to single-handedly save the three-toed sloth from extinction." But if I can point to specific contributions I have made in the past, and show how they align with specific goals to serve the community or people in need or the environment, then it would still make sense to talk about those.

CN: Absolutely. Every well-supported sincere statement that paints a positive, vivid, and consistent verbal picture is helpful. The most important thing is to help the admissions office get a sense of you as a person.

TN: What is the second common theme you think applicants should be careful to avoid?

CN: A second element common to many personal statements that, at least in my opinion, doesn't really do much to set them apart is a declaration along the lines of "All my life I've wanted to be (or my parents, family, or friends have said I should be) a lawyer." There's no doubt the statement is true for many applicants. And here, too, applicants may reasonably imagine that admissions officers will be appropriately impressed by an apparently lifelong commitment to pursuing a legal career. What may come as a surprise to those applicants, though, is that many of their future professors do not necessarily share their view that the exclusive (or even primary) purpose of law school is simply to train you to become a practising lawyer. Canadian law schools are academic rather than vocational institutions. Canadian law schools are all university faculties, after all. And the university, traditionally, has been distinguished as an institution of *non-vocational* higher learning. Of course, law schools also have an essential role to play as professional schools. These twin objectives have some interesting implications for Canadian law schools. (We'll have much more to say about that in chapter 4.)

TN: Well not to brag, but I've been told I'm great at arguing by my mother and should be a lawyer. But I guess I'll leave that out. For the sake of argument.

Summing Up

So if your stats seem to fall at least roughly within the ranges on the chart in Appendix A, that's great. Of course, that still doesn't mean you are guaranteed admission. Many law schools have to turn down hundreds – even thousands – of very strong applicants every year who would probably have done just fine in law school and in the legal profession, too, if they had been admitted. Happily, though, *not* falling within the ranges on the chart doesn't guarantee rejection either. The admissions process, as most schools emphasize, is more "holistic" than a simple numbers game (although, make no mistake, the numbers certainly matter a lot – especially at some schools).

Assembling this chart was useful to me mainly because it can be costly to submit large number of applications. If there doesn't seem to be any reasonable prospect of being admitted at a particular school, it may make more sense to spend your time, attention, and application fees on other schools instead.

The Application Process

So how do you apply? Let's begin with Ontario, where almost half of Canada's common law schools (and more than half of first-year law school spaces) are located. If you are applying to any (or all) of Ontario's eight law schools, you have to use a third-party system called the Ontario Law School Application Service (OLSAS). OLSAS is run through the Ontario University Application Centre (OUAC). Any of you who applied to an Ontario university for an undergraduate degree program will be familiar with this system. If you didn't go to university in Ontario, do not worry. The system is very straightforward and easy to use. It does make it quite easy to apply to the Ontario schools, and honestly, since all the Ontario schools use this same system, it can be tempting, at least for Ontario residents, to limit themselves to applying only to the Ontario schools. However, as we mentioned earlier, just as it can make sense for applicants from outside Ontario to apply to Ontario law schools, there are many good reasons for Ontario applicants to consider applying to one or more of the outstanding Canadian law schools outside of Ontario.

The OLSAS System for Ontario Law School Applications

To use the OLSAS system, you simply need to create an OLSAS account online through the OUAC website.[9]

Once you've created your OLSAS account, the system allows you to upload all of your information in one place. Whether you end up applying to just one Ontario school or to all eight, you only need to upload your transcripts, your LSAT number, your "sketch/verifiers" (which I explain below), and the contact information for your referees once. Not all law schools require referees, while some require two and others as many as three. Once you input your referees' email addresses, the system then sends an automated email message to them with a link to a reference form for the referees to fill out.

9 See online at https://www.ouac.on.ca/guide/olsas-guide.

OLSAS provides specific instructions about how to upload your transcripts, including the special steps to be taken by students who went to schools outside of Ontario and outside of Canada. Once you've uploaded your LSAT number to OLSAS, OLSAS then gets your LSAT score directly from LSAC (the Law School Admission Council), the non-profit corporation that administers the LSAT.

The OLSAS Sketch

One part of the OLSAS application that is the same for every school in Ontario is the applicant's "sketch." The sketch is like a résumé. Applicants applying in the general admission category are specifically told not to upload a separate résumé. You may be tempted to upload one anyway, since the OLSAS system does make it possible to do so. But don't. Admissions offices will be interested to see you demonstrate that you can read carefully and follow instructions accurately, and they won't look at your résumé anyway, no matter how brilliant it is. Instead, concentrate on filling in the online "sketch" system on OLSAS to highlight your relevant work experience and other accomplishments.

You may include a maximum of 32 entries. The entries are divided into six specific categories, such as "work experience," "extracurriculars," "volunteer," and so on. The categories appear in a drop-down menu. Now, for many applicants 32 entries might not seem like a lot of room. But remember, law schools are not typically interested in anything you did before university. That can be a little disheartening if you were an overachiever in high school but spent most of your time at university alone buried in books in the library. You may be sorely tempted to make sure the admissions people know that you were not only a straight A student in high school, but that you also volunteered with underprivileged kids, starred in the high school musical production, captained the basketball team, and wrote two original plays that were workshopped and performed by a local theatre group or whatever. You get it.

Unfortunately, as important, worthwhile, and genuinely impressive as all of these accomplishments might be, none of that will do much to enhance your law school application. So there's really no point using up any of your precious 32 entries listing highlights of your luminous high school career. But there is one possible loophole. If you think something from your high school years is *really* important, or if you did something incredibly outstanding while you happened to be in high school (like winning a gold medal in the Olympics, say, or participating in a recent moon landing), you can mention that special triumph in your personal essay, which we discuss in the next section.

For each of your entries you must identify a "verifier" – a person who can be contacted directly by each law school to confirm that your entry is true. A verifier isn't like a referee. They don't have to be able to say anything about your performance or talk about your character or your abilities or your potential. They don't even have to have known you well or for any particular length of time. They just have to be able to validly confirm that the particular activity or achievement that you have included in your sketch is true.

It might seem annoying to be required try to find a verifier for every single item on in your sketch. Finding a verifier for the role you played in student-run organizations, for example, can sometimes be especially challenging since the student leaders with whom you worked may have since graduated. But it is important. Law school admissions offices know that résumé inflation has become a real problem, and honest applicants shouldn't be at a disadvantage. Make sure you contact your verifiers before including their names and contact details on your application. It's a simple courtesy, but it can also be helpful to remind them about the activity or achievement that they have been asked to verify, especially if it was more than a few years ago. Also be sure you take the verifier process seriously. You may be thinking, there is no way law schools can check every single verifier on every single application they receive. You're probably right. But as one admissions officer at an Ontario law school explained in a presentation on applying to law school, though they don't check every detail on every application, they do conduct random spot checks on roughly 10 per cent of the applications. And consider that there would be no reason for a school to verify the accuracy of your application unless you were highly likely to be admitted. So the risk of getting caught making a false claim may only be "an inch wide" but it is a "mile deep." You simply can't jeopardize your application over something so easily avoidable. If your application happens to be one that is chosen for a random check and the law school either can't contact your verifiers or your verifiers can't confirm your entry, that would be just about the worst imaginable reason to not get into law school.

So do the work. Be 100 percent honest in your application. You might think the admissions committee will be more impressed if you just pad your sketch (a little). But just like an Instagram post that has been photoshopped, everyone can tell and it just ruins the rest of your feed. So certainly put your best foot forward, but don't exaggerate about your shoe size. And get an appropriate verifier for every single entry. I would suggest writing out every sketch and verifier you plan to use before actually starting the application. Then reach out to your verifiers, and reach out early – as soon as you have decided you want to apply. People are very busy. When I first considered applying, one of my potential verifiers took a full month to get back to me to confirm they would be able to verify one of my entries if I did eventually decide to apply. If you wait until just before the application deadline date to contact verifiers, it may well be too late.

Completing the basic application information on OLSAS is very straightforward and probably the easiest part of the process. It takes time, but you don't need to finish everything in a single session. You can begin, then pause at any time to take a break because the system lets you save your work in progress. However, it is important to remember that you cannot make any changes once you submit the application. SO DO NOT SUBMIT THE APPLICATION UNTIL YOU ARE TOTALLY HAPPY WITH IT.

Personal Essay

While most of the application materials submitted through OLSAS are identical for all Ontario schools, there are a handful of items that are tailored specifically to individual schools. Therefore, once you pick the school or schools you want to apply to, you will find a section to upload school-specific submissions. Each school is different, but most ask for some type of personal essay. You will not be able to upload the essay here as a document created using your own word processing program. Instead, there is an answer box on the OLSAS form into which you will have to directly type your essay. The length of the personal essay varies by school, and the maximum length is specified in "characters" rather than words. That makes a big difference . . . 4,000 characters is a lot more restrictive than 4,000 words.

Apart from differences in the length of essays, some schools have specific requirements for their personal essay while other schools don't. The specific instructions for each school's essay appear above the word box. All of these essay instructions can also be found on the schools' individual websites, so you can actually get started on drafting your personal essay even before you've started your application.

It can be an exhausting exercise writing even one personal essay, let alone eight (or 18, if you are one of those handful of people who decides to apply to every English-language common law school in Canada). So, naturally, it would be easier if you could just use the same essay for every school. But should you?

That's entirely up to you. But be careful. Read the instructions for each school carefully, and if you plan to use the same basic essay for each school (perhaps with some minor variations), triple check that you don't, mistakenly, tell the admissions office at Law School A that it has been your lifelong dream to attend Law School B. I know it sounds foolish and obvious, but when you're tired and working on multiple drafts of different essays it can be easy to make a mistake.

I attended a law school application seminar where one law school admissions officer said that with thousands of applications to vet, if your essay mistakenly refers to the wrong law school, they will automatically reject it. Now that seems reductive to me, and perhaps this was just a bluff intended to frighten people into redoubling their proofreading efforts. But why take the chance? It is an easy mistake to avoid. So just be careful.

Your personal essay is your time to show the law school who you really are and why you would be a great addition to their incoming class. It's a sort of one-sided interview on paper, rather than in person. Be sure to make the most of it.

Don't Miss the Application Deadline

It is important to make sure you submit your law school application before the deadline. For Ontario schools, the application deadline for the class entering in September is usually the beginning of November of the previous year. (So, for example, in 2024, the deadline to apply for admission in September 2025 was November 1, 2024. You can find the deadline by clicking "Key Dates" on the OUAC/OLSAS website.) Even if you completed every part of the application before the deadline, you must make sure to actually submit the application. Once you've submitted, your submission will be confirmed by email.

Law Schools Outside Ontario

Though Ontario has more law schools than any other province, there are many other great common law schools you can apply to in Canada outside of Ontario that are not covered by the

OLSAS system. That means you will need to apply to each one of those schools individually.

For each Canadian common law school outside of Ontario, you can apply through the school's website/portal. Each of these schools requires slightly different documents and information. However, most schools will require transcripts for all university courses, a personal essay, references, your LSAC number (for your LSAT score), and some form of résumé. If you are using the same references for these out-of-Ontario schools that you used on your OLSAS application, it would be a good idea to remind your referees that they will receive multiple reference requests to which they will be asked to respond. Otherwise, a referee might mistakenly assume that once they had submitted their reference through the OLSAS system it will be transmitted to all Canadian law schools, both within and outside Ontario.

Once you've applied it is good to check in to each university's online application portal to make sure all your documents are submitted and your application is complete. The application period for most schools from outside Ontario is open until December of the year before or January of the calendar year for which students are applying for entry that September. I did see one school outside Ontario that was open for application until March, but that is very unusual. For the most part, the application periods were closed before February.

Application Fees

Once information has been submitted to OLSAS, every Ontario school can potentially access it. However, OLSAS provides an option that lets you choose which schools you want to apply to.

Among other things, that decision will affect how much you will have to pay in application fees. You could select all eight. However, in addition to the initial $200 OLSAS charges you to apply through their system, there is also a $115 charge for each school you apply to. (These were the fees as of November 2024.) So, if you wanted to apply to all eight Ontario schools, the total cost would come to $1,120 (not including the cost of obtaining transcripts from your undergraduate university). The cost of obtaining transcripts will vary by school. In the case of my undergraduate university (the University of Toronto) the cost was $18 per transcript. Since you only need to upload one transcript to OLSAS, which is then available to every Ontario school to which you apply, you will only need to pay for a single transcript.

In addition to the application and transcript fees, you will need to take the standardized LSAT, discussed in the next chapter. The LSAT fee, as of 2024, was US $238. Many students also choose to take an LSAT preparation course, and the cost of those courses can range from $500 to a potentially budget-breaking $2,000+. So the cost of applying to law school isn't chump change.

LSAC does offer a fee waiver program for students in need. The LSAC website includes all the details about how to apply for this waiver if you're eligible and what fees will be waived. Certain schools also offer their own application fee waiver programs. For example, the University of Toronto works with OLSAS to waive the fees of students in financial need. Again, all of this information on how to apply or to determine waiver eligibility is on the website.

Most schools outside of Ontario charge individual application fees, ranging from $75 to $125, depending on the school.

Obviously, applying to a large number of schools increases your chances of getting in. You could maximize your chances of admission by applying to every school in the country, but that would cost over $2,000. More importantly, it takes a lot of time and energy to complete each application and, in the end, you may not actually be able to manage a move to a law school that is hundreds (or even thousands) of kilometres away from your permanent home. If you're like me and working a full-time job while applying, or if you are still in university, trying to find time to complete applications between writing papers and preparing for exams, it might be very difficult to complete a multitude of law school applications. Trying to apply to every school by the application deadline could also backfire if you spread yourself too thin to put your best foot forward on every application.

Appendix A: Application Information for English-Language Common Law School Programs in Canada[1]

University	Number of Applicants (Approx.)	Class Size (First Year) (Approx.)	Average GPA/Percentage (Approx.)	Average LSAT (Approx.)
1. University of Alberta Faculty of Law[2]	1,275	185	3.8/4.0	161
2. Allard School of Law – UBC[3]	1,500	200	84 %	166
3. Bora Laskin Faculty of Law – Lakehead University[4]	678	65	Not provided[5]	Not provided

1 The information in this chart is based in part on information from law schools' official websites and in part on information from third party websites. So readers should remember to trust the internet here as much as you usually do. Some websites had up-to-date statistics, while some did not. The numbers that appear here were based on research completed in early 2025, but the information on all of these websites is frequently updated and amended. Current numbers could be materially different from the numbers that appear here. These numbers are also approximations. The purpose of this chart is therefore only to help you get a rough general idea on competitive application statistics, but they are not intended to be relied upon.

2 https://www.lsac.org/choosing-law-school/find-law-school/canadian-law-schools/university-alberta-faculty.

3 https://allard.ubc.ca/programs/juris-doctor-jd-program/admissions/jd-admissions-program-eligibility-and-requirements; https://allard.ubc.ca/programs/juris-doctor-jd-program/frequently-asked-questions.

4 https://www.lakeheadu.ca/programs/departments/law/admissions/law-admission-questions; https://www.lsac.org/choosing-law-school/find-law-school/canadian-law-schools/bora-laskin-faculty-law.

5 The Bora Laskin Law School's official website says they do not provide LSAT scores and median GPAs. However, according to the OLSAS website, someone with a B+ average overall and an A- in the last two years would be considered a competitive applicant.

Appendix A: Application Information for English-Language Common Law School Programs in Canada *(continued)*

4. University of Calgary Faculty of Law[6]	1,355	128	3.7/4.0	164
5. Dalhousie University Schulich School of Law[7]	1,300	170	3.7/4.3	161–164
6. University of Manitoba Faculty of Law[8]	665	107	3.97/4.5	161
7. McGill University Faculty of Law[9]	1,132	180	3.8/4.0	164
8. University of New Brunswick Faculty of Law[10]	715	92	3.8/4.3	159
9. Osgoode Hall Law School – York University[11]	3,110	315	3.7/4.0	85th percentile

6 https://law.ucalgary.ca/future-students/admissions-jd-programs/assessment-of-applications.

7 https://www.lsac.org/choosing-law-school/find-law-school/canadian-law-schools/dalhousie-university; https://www.dal.ca/faculty/law/admissions/jd-admissions.html; https://www.dal.ca/faculty/law/admissions/jd-admissions/how-to-apply.html.

8 https://www.lsac.org/choosing-law-school/find-law-school/canadian-law-schools/university-manitoba; https://law.robsonhall.com/wp-content/uploads/2022/09/Web-Stats-202290.pdf.

9 https://www.mcgill.ca/law/bcl-jd/program-description/student-body-and-alumni-data; https://www.mcgill.ca/law/bcl-jd/admissions-guide/eligibility.

10 https://www.unb.ca/fredericton/law/future/admissions/index.html; https://www.oxfordseminars.ca/LSAT/lsat_profiles.php.

11 https://www.osgoode.yorku.ca/programs/juris-doctor/juris-doctor-admissions/eligibility-requirements; https://www.uottawa.ca/faculty-law/common-law/admissions/evaluation-applications.

Appendix A: Application Information for English-Language Common Law School Programs in Canada

10. University of Ottawa Faculty of Law[12]	2,637	320	80%	158
11. Queens University Faculty of Law[13]	2900	216	3.7/4.0	160
12. Thompson Rivers University Faculty of Law[14]	Not available	124	3.7–3.85/4.0	158
13. University of Toronto Faculty of Law[15]	2,607	232	3.91/4.0	167
14. Lincoln Alexander School of Law – Toronto Metropolitan University[16]	2,521	152	Not available	Not available
15. University of Victoria Faculty of Law[17]	1,000	110	3.84/4.0	165
16. Western University Faculty of Law[18]	2,551	198	3.65/4.0	162

12 https://www.uottawa.ca/faculty-law/common-law/admissions/evaluation-applications.

13 https://law.queensu.ca/frequently-asked-questions.

14 https://www.lsac.org/choosing-law-school/find-law-school/canadian-law-schools/thompson-rivers-university.

15 https://www.law.utoronto.ca/about/fact-sheet#Profile.

16 https://www.lsac.org/choosing-law-school/find-law-school/canadian-law-schools/toronto-metro; https://www.torontomu.ca/law/admissions/admission-requirements.

17 https://www.uvic.ca/law/admissions/jdadmissionfaqs/index.php; https://www.uvic.ca/law/assets/docs/lsat-gpa-demographic-chart-2021.pdf.

18 https://law.uwo.ca/future_students/jd_admissions/class_profiles.html.

Appendix A: Application Information for English-Language Common Law School Programs in Canada *(continued)*

17. University of Windsor Faculty of Law[19]	2,000	165	Not available	Not available
18. University of Saskatchewan College of Law[20]	1120	126	3.7/4.0	159

19 https://www.uwindsor.ca/law/1163/windsor-law-admissions-faq.

20 https://www.lsac.org/choosing-law-school/find-law-school/canadian-law-schools/university-saskatchewan.

3

the LSAT laugh

Introduction

1948.

Why is this year relevant to an aspiring law school applicant, you might wonder? Well, when you are applying to most Canadian common law schools, you will have to write the dreaded standardized Law School Admission Test (LSAT). And the LSAT was first officially administered to law school applicants in 1948. Why do you have to write the LSAT to apply to law school? We'll defer that question for the moment. What I would like to do first is provide you with some history of the LSAT and also some personal experiences with the test. I have had the "pleasure" of taking the LSAT (more than once, but who's counting), so I have some recent hands-on experience with what you may come to think of as a multiple-choice menace that may be a test of your patience as much as your aptitude and may well become the bane of your existence. (Or at least it was the bane of mine.)

Your "objective" opinion of the value of the LSAT is likely to depend on how well you personally tend to perform on standardized tests. People who are good at standardized tests are often convinced that they are the best indicators of true intelligence and an important way to screen out students whose high grade point averages are simply the product of low university academic standards and blatant grade inflation. People who are not good at standardized tests are equally convinced that multiple-choice tests reveal nothing about a person's creativity, genuine intelligence, and aptitude for complex interpersonal tasks that are essential for success in any human endeavour. Even worse, they may be biased in various ways that mean they are not only worthless, but positively harmful.

The LSAT's limitations are no secret to law school admissions officers. Many law schools in the United States have, in fact, experimented with using alternatives to the LSAT for admissions purposes. For example, many of the most well-known US law schools, including Harvard, Yale, Stanford, Columbia, University of Chicago, New York University, Northwestern Pritzker, and Duke, all allow applicants to choose between completing either the LSAT or the Graduate Record Examination (GRE), a standardized test often used for graduate school admissions. Several other schools expand the list of alternative eligible standardized tests to include not only the LSAT and the GRE but also the Graduate Management Admission Test (GMAT), the standardized test usually taken by applicants for Master of Business Administration (MBA) programs. US law schools that will accept the GMAT in lieu of the LSAT or GRE currently include Penn Carey (University of Pennsylvania), Cornell, and Georgetown.

Still, for applicants applying to most Canadian common law schools, the LSAT is still mandatory. The one distinguished exception is the McGill University Faculty of Law. McGill does not require applicants to take the LSAT because McGill offers a bilingual program to which a significant number of applicants whose first language is French apply. Since the LSAT is offered only in English, McGill's Faculty of Law has stated that "we believe it would be disadvantageous to the significant proportion of applicants and admitted students who indicate French as a first language to require, as a matter of eligibility, a test that is offered only in English."[1] However, McGill also requires any applicant who has written the LSAT – including applicants who were required to write the LSAT to be eligible to apply to other law schools – to disclose their LSAT scores to McGill "regardless of whether the LSAT may, in their own estimation, strengthen or weaken their candidacy."[2] Accordingly, as a practical matter, unless an applicant is applying to McGill and no other Canadian common law school, the LSAT is also a factor in the McGill law school admission process.

You may be asking how answering multiple-choice questions about turgid passages from *Scientific American* and the reasoning process of fictional decision makers is related to the study or practice of law. I mean, you could even go further and ask what does *any* of the LSAT have to do with the study or

1 McGill University, Faculty of Law, "Application Process for BCL/JD Degree Program," online: https://www.mcgill.ca/study/2024-2025/faculties/law/undergraduate/ug_law_application_procedures#booknode-1475.
2 *Ibid.*

practice of law? Actually, I *am* asking. Why do law school applicants have to take the LSAT? Where did it come from? And how did this particular US standardized test achieve such credibility among Canadian law school admissions officers?

Not surprisingly, the company that administers the LSAT makes strong claims for its predictive power. Their website boasts that "Studies have consistently shown the LSAT to be the single best predictor of first-year law school performance, even better than undergraduate grade-point average."[3]

Still, the designers of the LSAT themselves seem to have had second thoughts about the accuracy of the test over the years, because there have been many changes to the LSAT since it was first introduced. We discuss some these changes later in this chapter.

The LSAT: A "Capacity" Test

But let's first consider the threshold question: What was the LSAT originally intended for? In a 1948 article in the *Journal of Legal Education*,[4] Willis Reese, who was then a prominent professor at the Columbia Law School,[5] explained that the LSAT began as an experimental "capacity" (or aptitude) test adopted by a number of leading US law schools. The goal was to make the law school admissions procedure more "civilized." It would

3 LSAC website, "The LSAT," online: https://www.lsac.org/lsat.

4 Willis Reese, "The Standard Law School Admission Test" (1948) 1:1 J Legal Educ 124.

5 See Columbia Law School, "Who Was Willis LM Reese?" online: https://www.law.columbia.edu/news/archive/who-was-willis-lm-reese.

be far better, it was thought, to identify up front the people most likely to succeed in law school rather than continue what Professor Reese described as the outdated and "barbarous practice of admitting nearly everyone with a college degree and then excluding a large percentage of the class at the end of the first year."[6]

That last point is very telling. There is a famous story that older lawyers – from many different law schools – repeat, often claiming they were present and witnessed it first-hand. According to this story, on the first day of class the dean or the course professor would say to all the assembled first-year law students: "Look to your left and look to your right. Next year, one of you won't be here." It is unlikely that these words were ever heard anywhere except in people's imagination. It reminds me of the line from R.L. Stine's old *Goosebumps* books (remember those?): "It happened to a friend of a friend of mine." But even if the story isn't literally true, it does convey the sort of harshness of law school failure rates that were apparently common in the bad old pre-LSAT days Professor Reese was referring to.

There were a few other justifications for the LSAT, too. For example, some defenders of the LSAT have argued that a standardized test helps make law schools more meritocratic[7] and

---

6 Reese, above note 4 at 124.

7 The term "meritocracy" is usually seen today as a desirable way of organizing society – a much fairer, even more democratic, alternative to systems based on accidents of birth or other unearned privileges. However, the author who originally coined the term "meritocracy," Alan Fox, didn't share this view at all. Fox was actually highly critical of the idea of presumed "merit" ever becoming an appropriate basis for organizing society (see Alan Fox, "Class and Inequality," *Socialist Commentary* [May 1956] 11). The author who probably did more than anyone else

less elitist. If everyone is required to write a standardized aptitude test to be considered for admission, deserving students from less affluent backgrounds and no influential personal "contacts" will have the same chance of admission to prestigious schools as their less competent but wealthier and more "well-connected" classmates. Tests like the LSAT could, therefore, help level the public-private-prep-school playing field.

More recently, however, standardized tests have been criticized on the basis of systemic concerns. As the LSAT became increasingly important for admissions decisions, applicants looked for ways to get a leg up on their fellow applicants by preparing for the LSAT. A whole industry grew up around publishing "practice tests" and running LSAT preparation courses. The preparation courses can be quite expensive. Are they worth the money? If the LSAT is really a test of raw aptitude for law school study, then it shouldn't be possible to increase your score significantly by preparing for it – for instance, by taking an expensive LSAT prep course. But those prep courses do claim that they can substantially increase your score (or your next course is free!). So a cynic might be tempted to say that either the LSAT prep courses are a sham or the LSAT itself is. (I'm not one of those cynics, of course.)

---

to popularize the term, Michael Young, was a socialist who condemned the idea of meritocracy, particularly as perpetuated by the British educational system, as a vicious organizing principle that could be manipulated by the ruling classes to unfairly perpetuate their positions of privilege while leaving others demoralized and disaffected in ways that were far worse than what occurred under alternative overtly privilege-based social systems. In a meritocracy, Young lamented, "No underclass has ever been left as morally naked as that." See Michael Young, "Down with Meritocracy," *The Guardian* (29 June 2001). For a more recent critique of meritocracy by Harvard University philosopher Michael J. Sandel, see *The Tyranny of Merit: What's Become of the Common Good?* (New York: Farrar, Straus and Giroux, 2020).

What Does the LSAT Have to Do with Studying Law?

The LSAT is intended to test capacity or aptitude, not knowledge. But aptitude for what, exactly?

No multiple-choice standardized test is likely to be able to determine whether or not someone is likely to become a successful lawyer. The complex interpersonal, negotiating, advocacy, client management, and other skills that distinguish the greatest lawyers will never be revealed through a series of multiple-choice questions about obscure reading passages and logic games that seem to have come straight from the *New York Times* Games app.

But the LSAT doesn't claim to be a test for identifying good lawyers. It is a test that is supposed to help identify people who are likely to succeed at law school. There is apparently some evidence that high LSAT test scores – especially when combined with high undergraduate GPAs – do have a significant (but not perfect) correlation with high first-year law school grades. In some ways, this correlation might be expected. Since, as we discuss in chapter 8, final examinations are often a major part of law school grades, some of that correlation may simply be due to the fact that people who do well on a long standardized test like the LSAT may have lower exam anxiety than those who don't do as well. But whether the LSAT is really measuring aptitude for learning or simply aptitude for formal test taking, for practical purposes it doesn't really matter. The LSAT has long been, and still is, just one of the necessary hoops most law school applicants in Canada must jump through.

The Format of the LSAT

The original 1948 LSAT was even more brutal than the current version. It took all day to complete and had ten sections.[8] (And I thought the modern three-hour test with four sections plus a writing requirement was a bit much.) The LSAT has frequently been changed throughout its history.

Even as recently as five years ago the LSAT format was very different from today's test. And it's still undergoing some changes. On July 30, 2024, the people that administer the LSAT introduced something called "LSAT argumentative writing."[9] This is an unscored section that will take the place of the LSAT writing prompt, an unscored writing section that we will discuss in a little more detail below. (The reason these sections are unscored is that they are simply intended to provide law schools with a short sample of the applicant's writing produced under standardized test conditions. The law school admissions officers can then decide for themselves how, if at all, they wish to evaluate that writing sample when they are making admissions decisions.)

In August 2024, the LSAT also removed the analytical reasoning section of the test. This is the test section some people refer to as "logic games." As a result of these recent changes, the test going forward will have three scored sections and one unscored section (as well as the unscored argumentative

---

8 LSAC, "Mission & History: Our Mission," online: https://www.lsac.org/about/mission-history.

9 LSAC, "LSAT Argumentative Writing," online: https://www.lsac.org/lsat/about/lsat-argumentative-writing.

writing section). The three scored sections will consist of two sets of questions on logical reasoning and one on reading comprehension. The unscored sections will include one multiple-choice section of either logical reasoning or reading comprehension questions plus the argumentative writing requirement. Though test takers are also required to complete the unscored argumentative writing section, it doesn't have to be completed right after the test or even on the same day.

The Law School Admission Council (LSAC), the body that administers the LSAT, claims that this format change won't make a difference to test takers' scores.[10] That seems a little strange to me. After all, if it's true that the changes won't result in any significant score changes, why is the change being made? Alternatively, if the new format is being adopted because it is thought to be an even better predictor of law school performance than prior versions of the LSAT, shouldn't we expect scores to be different, too? Luckily (for me at least), I had the chance to write the LSAT when analytical reasoning (or "logic games"), my best and favourite section, were still a part of the test.

The scoring of the test has changed as well. In 1948 scores were based on a 200–800 point scale. Student scores were reported both as a number (between 200 and 800) and a corresponding "percentile," indicating how well that student scored

---

10 According to the LSAC website: "The August 2024 update is backed by rigorous research, including analysis of over 200,000 test sessions, ensuring the test's reliability and validity. *The research confirms that the revised approach would have virtually no impact on overall scores.*" (Emphasis added.) LSAC, "Changes Are Coming to the LSAT in August 2024," online: https://www.lsac.org/lsat/lsat-changes-coming-august-2024.

relative to all of the other LSAT test takers. A seventy-fifth percentile score, for example, meant that your score was higher than 75 percent of all test takers.

That 800 point scoring system was used for a number of years. Then, in 1981, the scale was changed. The highest achievable score changed dramatically from 800 to 48, and the lowest score changed from 200 to 10. The 10–48 point scale was used for the next ten years.

The scoring system changed again in 1992 to the current 120–180 point scale. The point scores alone, however, mean very little without an understanding of the corresponding percentiles. A small difference in point scores can represent a significant difference in percentiles. So, for example, during the period 2021–2024, a score of 153 on the LSAT would place a test taker in the fiftieth percentile, right in the middle of the test-taking pack. This means that about 50 percent of test takers scored below 153. Yet a score of just 13 points higher, at 166, would place a test taker in the elite ranks of the ninetieth percentile. Only 10 percent of test takers received a score above 166.[11]

In addition to the various changes that have been made to the content of the LSAT and to the scoring scales over the years, perhaps the most significant change to the LSAT has been the change in test-taking format. At one time, all students taking the LSAT wrote by hand, in person, on the same date, at large common testing centres all across the United States and Canada (such as in university lecture halls or hotel convention rooms). But in 2019 the LSAT became digital. Students still

11 LSAC, "LSAT Percentiles 2021–2024," online (pdf): https://www.lsac.org/document-library/596.

wrote the LSAT in large examination rooms with other test takers, but now on the day of the test every test taker was provided a computer tablet and a stylus. There were no more scantrons, question booklets, or number 2 pencils. Although test takers were given scrap paper to make notes, all test answers were submitted electronically on the touchscreen tablet.

One minor incidental effect of the new digital test format was that it prevented any backtracking. Test takers were given 35 minutes to complete each section. Once the time to complete a section expired, that was it: the tablet immediately moved on to the next section, making it impossible even to offer guesses to unanswered questions on the previous section.

When the digital version of the LSAT was launched, a major change was also introduced to the writing component of the test. Prior to the launch of the digital version of the LSAT, the test included an unscored writing section consisting of a writing "prompt," in which the test taker was presented with a hypothetical scenario that posed some sort of dilemma (usually an ethical dilemma). Following the description of this dilemma, two alternative solutions were proposed. Test takers were required to choose one of the two offered solutions and write an essay defending their chosen solution. They were given 35 minutes to complete this writing assignment. Test takers would be required to complete the writing section immediately after they had finished the multiple-choice LSAT questions, while still in the same testing room and under the watchful eye of the same test proctor.

When the digital version of the LSAT was released, the LSAT writing requirement was revised. The writing section no longer had to be completed immediately after the multiple-choice questions. Instead, test takers could now choose to complete the writing section from their own home and submit their completed work at any time up to a year from the day they completed the multiple-choice LSAT questions. As of August 2024, the writing section of the LSAT has changed again. The test taker will still be able to complete the writing section after the exam and from their own home; however, instead of the former writing "prompts," which asked test takers to choose either side of a specified argument to defend, the new "argumentative writing" section calls on writers to frame and defend their own thesis.

Allowing the test to be written in the test taker's own home meant new proctoring technology was needed. The system LSAC uses to administer the writing section at home is called ProctorU. This system provides each test taker an online proctor. The proctor must have remote access to the test taker's computer. (The test taker must grant access to the proctor at the beginning of the test to be eligible to take the test.)

The system requires the test taker to do a camera scan of the room before starting the test to make sure there is no one else in the room and to ensure that are no "illegal" materials available to the test taker. The online proctor also has access to the test taker's computer web cam, which must remain on throughout the entire test. The proctor watches through your webcam while you write the entire test. If the proctor notices something suspicious – furtive glances by the student, for example, that may be attempts to look at a stealthily concealed cell phone – the proctor can notify the student immediately by sending a message to their computer screen. The proctor will also make comments about any observed suspicious behaviour on the student's test. Any comments of this sort by the proctor can adversely affect the test taker's score, or could even disqualify the test from being marked at all.

When the LSAT was revised to digital format, the writing requirement was still considered an essential part of the test, and law schools couldn't accept an applicant's LSAT score until the writing section had been submitted. Once completed, the writing section now would remain valid for five years. So if an applicant chose to take the LSAT again within that five-year period, they wouldn't be required to complete the writing section again.

In March 2020, as we remember all too well, the COVID-19 pandemic prompted governments around the world to introduce a series of lockdowns to prevent the spread of the virus. It was no longer possible to administer the LSAT to large groups of test takers in large test centres. To deal with these unusual circumstances, LSAC created something called the LSAT-Flex, a computer-based version of the LSAT designed to be taken securely in a test taker's own home and proctored electronically using ProctorU (the same program used to monitor completion of the LSAT writing requirement).

The COVID-19 version of the LSAT included only three sections: logical reasoning, reading comprehension, and analytical reasoning. Unlike earlier versions of the LSAT, which contained additional "experimental" sections that were not factored into a test taker's score, the test was written with no breaks and all three of the LSAT-Flex sections were scored. The writing component worked the same way as in the previous version of the LSAT: Test takers were given up to one year to complete and submit it.

As pandemic lockdown restrictions eased, the format of the LSAT was changed once again. It is no longer mandatory to take the test in person at a testing centre. You are now allowed to take the LSAT at home, just like during the COVID-19 lockdowns. However, you are also given the option to write in person if you prefer. If you want to write the test in person, the in-person LSATs are now administered by a third-party company called Prometric. Prometric administers multiple standardized tests and exams, not just the LSAT, so it is possible that you may have taken a test administered by this company before. Prometric provides the test location, the room, and the computer that you take the test on. They also administer the various security checks you have to satisfy before being allowed to take the test, and they record when you start and finish the test. The test itself, however, is still provided by LSAC.

The test is no longer administered on a tablet. Instead, it is administered on a desktop computer provided at the test site. Once in the secure room, you log onto LSAC'S website. From there, you access LSAC's LawHub system. If you have signed up for the LSAT, a prompt appears in LawHub on the exact date and time you signed up for the LSAT. Once the prompt appears you can begin the test. If you are writing the test from home you go through the same ProctorU system that was explained earlier in the chapter.

Can You Study for the LSAT?

Everyone taking the LSAT wants to know how to get the highest possible score. What can you do to try to improve your LSAT score and thus increase your chances of being admitted to law school? In theory, because the LSAT is supposed to test aptitude rather than knowledge, it shouldn't be possible to study for the LSAT. In fact, if it were possible to study for the LSAT, then the LSAT would seem to be testing something other than aptitude. But there is a big demand for LSAT preparation courses, and some law schools not only encourage prospective law students to take such courses, but even provide such courses for students who might not otherwise be able to afford the course fees.

Do these prep courses work? The companies that offer them certainly claim they do. And there has been some research suggesting that LSAT prep courses can have a significant positive impact on test takers' scores. For example, one study by scientists at the University of California (Berkeley) in 2012 concluded that LSAT test preparation courses actually changed the structure of the human brain in ways that improved reasoning.[12]

I don't know whether the structure of my brain has actually been changed, but from my own experience taking the LSAT I would suggest taking an LSAT prep course. There is nothing that can be memorized in advance that will help you perform better on the LSAT – it is mainly a logic and reading skills test, after all. So the only way to really "study" for the LSAT is to practise the type of questions found on the LSAT and learn some test-taking speed tricks. That is just the sort of practice LSAT prep courses offer.

Someone once suggested to me that writing the LSAT is a bit like running a marathon. (And not just because, like an exhausted marathon runner, you may feel horribly sick

12 Allyson P Mackey, Kirstie J Whitaker & Silvia A Bunge, "Experience-Dependent Plasticity in White Matter Microstructure: Reasoning Training Alters Structural Connectivity" (2012) 6 Frontiers in Neuroanatomy, online: https://www.frontiersin.org/journals/neuroanatomy/articles/10.3389/fnana.2012.00032/full.

immediately after you have finished the LSAT.) You definitely won't be able to finish a marathon if you don't train and practise. However, no matter how much training you do, if something unexpected goes wrong on the day of the race your training won't do much to overcome unpleasant surprises. So it's important to do many practice tests in advance if you want to increase your chances of doing well, but all the practice in the world won't necessarily mean you will excel on test day. I think it's important to remember to be kind to yourself. Standardized tests can be hard and demoralizing, and they are limited to testing a pretty narrow set of frankly highly unusual skills.

If you don't think your LSAT score is high enough for you to be admitted to your first-choice law school, you can always take the test again. In fact, you can take it up to seven times in total. So if you hear someone bragging about their 170 score, remember that you don't know how many times they took the test before they reached that impressive number.

Most Canadian law schools say they will consider only your highest LSAT score when assessing your application for admission. Since the LSAT is supposed to be an aptitude test, it makes sense that you might have one particularly bad day and perform below your ability, but it seems unlikely that you would somehow ever be able to score significantly above your "real" ability.

One other piece of advice I would offer to students who are still in university and planning to take the LSAT is to consider enrolling in a course in logic in your university's philosophy department. Philosophy, and particularly logic, teaches you how to evaluate the conclusions and the premises of an argument in a way that is similar to what is expected especially in the "logical reasoning" portions of the LSAT. Some of the approaches that an LSAT course instructor once recommended to me I had actually already learned in one of my first undergraduate philosophy courses.

Don't Let the LSAT Get the LAST Laugh

Finally, remember that the LSAT is not the LAST word. Most law schools try to take a holistic approach when evaluating applications, which means that although your LSAT score definitely matters, so do all the other unique components of your application and the distinct picture of you that emerges from the collage of all the parts of your application. So, of course, take all the steps you can to get the highest LSAT score possible. It is very important, and it must be taken seriously. But don't let a less-than-stellar LSAT score stop you from applying. The only way to know whether you can get admitted to law school is to apply. So, if you are committed to going to law school, don't be discouraged from applying by anyone who says "That's just not a high enough score."

Always, always, always apply.

Notes

The following sources were consulted in preparing this chapter. Readers may wish to consult one or more of these resources for more details:

Allyson P Mackey, Kirstie J Whitaker & Silvia A Bunge, "Experience-Dependent Plasticity in White Matter Microsctructure: Reasoning Training Alters Structural Connectivity" (2012) 6 Frontiers in Neuroanatomy, online: https://www.frontiersin.org/journals/neuroanatomy/articles/10.3389/fnana.2012.00032/full.

Willis Reese, "The Standard Law School Admission Test" (1948) 1:1 J Legal Educ 124.

Law School Expert, "Checking in on LSAT Changes and Trends," online (blog): https://www.lawschoolexpert.com/lsat-changes-trends.
LSAC, "The LSAT," online: https://www.lsac.org/lsat.
Manhattan Review, "Recent Changes to the LSAT," online: https://www.manhattanreview.com/lsat-changes.
Erin Mihalik, "The End of the LSAT?" Martindale-Avvo (29 June 2022), online (blog): https://www.martindale-avvo.com/blog/the-end-of-the-lsat.
Manhattan Review, "History of the LSAT," online: https://www.manhattanreview.com/lsat-history.

part three
what to expect at law school

4

law school, or lawyers' school?

Introduction

Well, you're still here after Part Two. I hope that means you are still interested (at least at this point) in putting a law school application forward. For most people, that means you are probably interested in learning how to eventually practise law. Here is where things get a little complicated.

As we mentioned in chapter 2, one of the things that may come as a surprise to law school applicants is that some law professors don't necessarily believe that the exclusive, or even main, purpose of law school is to train people to become practising lawyers. They point out that law schools are university faculties, and universities are not primarily institutions that specialize in practical, vocational training. Personally, I'm not sure that there is anything unusual about university programs combining academic and vocational aspects. What about university medical schools? Aren't they intended to train practising physicians, not simply academic researchers? And how about engineering faculties? Surely their goal is to graduate competent engineers, not to produce impractical theoreticians who know everything about, say, the philosophy of engineering but who lack the practical knowledge and skill to design safe bridges. I don't believe most law professors would disagree with the general idea that law school must provide an appropriate education for students planning to enter the practice of law. Nor would they disagree with the idea that law schools should bridge the practical and the theoretical. But it does seem as though there is ongoing debate about which side of the practical/theoretical divide should loom largest at the modern Canadian law school and to what degree.

TN: Why would law schools ever want to resist the characterization that, like other professional schools, they, too, are primarily (if not exclusively) professional schools preparing people – yes, even training people – to enter a particular profession?

CN: It is a complicated story. Certainly, all Canadian law schools – institutionally – do recognize the crucial importance of being accredited as professional schools by the bodies that govern the legal profession. Without that accreditation, they would not be very attractive to the best potential students and, if we're being honest, it is unlikely that they would be able to charge those students the high tuition fees commanded by most law schools across the country either. So law schools all well understand that they have a critical role to play in professional education that is distinctly different from, say, university departments of philosophy or classical studies. They also recognize, and are committed to playing, their indispensable role in preparing people to become competent, thoughtful, and ethical members of the legal profession. There is no doubt about that. But individual law professors – like professors in other faculties of the university – typically see themselves as scholars: people who occasionally talk about "the academy," and not when they are referring to the body responsible for awards bestowed in the American motion picture industry. Though they may also insist that they really are "lawyers" too, most of them have either never practised law or have practised law for such an insignificant period of time (perhaps no more than a year or two) that they barely progressed beyond the apprentice stage of professional practice themselves, and in many cases did so in the somewhat distant past.

TN: *But why aren't all law professors required to also practise or at least to have significant practice experience? Doesn't it make more sense to learn securities law from someone practising securities law or to learn about contracts from someone who has actually drafted contracts rather than to have someone stuck in a classroom who only knows – in theory – what a contract is? (No offence, by the way. And now you can't take offence because I've specifically said, "no offence.")*

CN: Many law professors don't regard the lack of significant legal practice experience as a deficiency at all. On the contrary. Some years ago, for example, a professor at a leading American law school went so far as to declare that legal practice experience actually would nearly disqualify a person from teaching at a law school.[1]

This is not some radical, modern (or postmodern) idea of the university law school. It is actually quite an old idea. Charles Eliot, the president of Harvard University who first appointed Christopher Columbus Langdell to be a professor at Harvard Law School and urged his election as the law school's first dean in 1870, said that Langdell had very much been of this view as well: "He was inclined to believe that success at the Bar or on the Bench was, in all probability, a disqualification for the functions of a professor of law."[2] This may seem all the more surprising since Langdell himself had come to the law school after a considerable period of time as a legal practitioner, although a famous critic of Langdell suggested that most of Langdell's years in practice were spent in the library, not the courtroom.[3]

Law students and some practising lawyers sometimes complain that at least some (and perhaps many) of their law school classes are too theoretical.[4] Some law professors, on the other hand, have just the opposite perspective. They worry that law schools are occasionally too focused on

---

1 Dina Awerbuch, "Professor Levinson Demystifies the Path to Legal Academia," *Harvard Law School Record* (19 October 2007).

2 Charles Eliot, "Langdell and the Law School" (1920) 33 Harv L Rev 518 at 520.

3 Jerome Frank, "What Constitutes a Good Legal Education?" (1933) 19:12 ABA J 723 at 723.

4 For example, see Kate Reder Sheikh, "What Law Schools Should Really Be Teaching" (August 15, 2022), online: https://www.mlaglobal.com/en/insights/articles/what-law-school-should-really-be-teaching?byconsultantorauthor-kate-reder-sheikh: "Law school could be a better experience. It could be more practical and could encompass the business of law more than it does. It could be less theoretical and more brass-tacks."

trying to produce "practice-ready" lawyers who are spending too much time trying to acquire nuts-and-bolts technical skills that will actually prove to have a very short useful life. Helping students develop deeper theoretical knowledge is not only more consistent with the traditional role of the university, they insist, but may also prove to be of much more enduring value for students. As a former colleague of mine used to put it, "There is nothing more practical than theory." There is also a question of institutional competence and comparative advantage: Practical lawyering skills can be taught far more efficiently and far more quickly in a hands-on practical environment after students have completed their foundational academic training in law.

But there is clearly an important role in university law schools for both theoretical and practical or "experiential" elements. Most Canadian legal educators are familiar with prominent reports about the state of law schools that have come to more or less opposite conclusions. In 1983, there was an influential report undertaken on Canadian law schools entitled *Law and Learning*.[5] Law professors often refer to this document as the "Arthurs Report" after the chair of the consultative group that produced the report, Professor Harry Arthurs. The Arthurs Report found significant shortcomings in the scholarly mission of Canadian law schools. As the report concludes, "The non-vocational

---

5 The Consultative Group on Research and Education in Law (Harry Arthurs, Chair), *Law and Learning: Report to the Social Sciences and Humanities Research Council of Canada* (Ottawa: Social Sciences and Humanities Research Council of Canada Information Division, 1983).

study of law as one of the humanities or social sciences is seldom undertaken."[6] Most of the research undertaken at law schools was doctrinal, rather than theoretical, and was "scattered" and influenced mainly by the priorities of governments and the legal profession rather than "the requirements of intellectual inquiry or societal development."[7] In short, law schools were falling short because they were too practical, too vocational, and too closely linked to the legal profession. A number of the Arthurs Report's key recommendations thus related to various ways of promoting more scholarly research at Canadian law schools.[8]

Now, compare this diagnosis and those recommendations with the conclusions and recommendations of another well-known report on legal education: the Carnegie Foundation Report titled *Educating Lawyers*.[9] The Carnegie Report acknowledges that law schools, "like other professional schools, are hybrid institutions"[10] with both scholarly and vocational missions. But, the authors observe (with apparent disapproval), over time "their academic genes have become dominant."[11] The solution? Among other things, law schools should, the report recommends, offer a more "integrated curriculum" that would, among other things, introduce "more facets of practice."[12] And the "common

6 *Ibid* at 153.
7 *Ibid* at 83.
8 *Ibid* at 157 ff.
9 William M Sullivan et al, *Educating Lawyers: Preparation for the Practice of Law* (Princeton, NJ: Carnegie Foundation for the Advancement of Teaching, 2007).
10 *Ibid* at 4.
11 *Ibid* at 4.
12 *Ibid* at 8.

core of legal education," the report recommends, "needs to be expanded to provide students substantial experience with practice as well as opportunities to wrestle with the issues of professionalism."[13] In short, law schools should embrace (as the American Bar Association has also mandated) more "experiential learning."[14]

It seems, from reviewing these sorts of contradictory reports, that everyone knows that law schools are either far too theoretical and impractical or far too practical and vocational.

So, as I hope you can see, the practice of law and the formal study of law have an interesting and delicate relationship. It is important to remember, too, that in many ways "law schools," as most readers of this book understand them, are comparatively new.

How Did We Get Here? (And Who Cares?)

TN: But lawyers have been around for a heck of a long time, haven't they? For centuries, in fact. So how can law schools be new?

CN: To answer that question, we need to briefly review the history of law schools. It is a worthwhile exercise, because if you understand that history it may be easier for you to understand something very important about modern

13 *Ibid* at 9.

14 American Bar Association, *2024–2025 ABA Standards and Rules of Procedure for Approval of Law Schools 2024–2025*, Standard 303(a)(3), online (pdf): https://www.americanbar.org/content/dam/aba/administrative/legal_education_and_admissions_to_the_bar/standards/2024-2025/2024-2025-standards-and-rules-for-approval-of-law-schools.pdf.

Canadian law schools: the ongoing (if often exaggerated) tension between the academic and the practical. Sometimes that tension lurks quietly beneath the surface; at other times, it is in very clear view.

We can gain interesting insights into the history of legal education by looking at early examples of books like this one, written for prospective law students. Books written for people about to embark on the study of law have been around for a long time. A very long time. There was a very well-known book on this topic, *Learning the Law*,[15] by an English legal scholar, Glanville Williams, first published in 1945 that is perhaps the most well-known twentieth-century example. An admiring reviewer said of the first edition of Williams's book that "Nothing quite like this has been attempted thereto."[16] But I must respectfully disagree. Some sources suggest that the first of these sorts of works was Samuel Warren's 1835 book, *A Popular and Practical Introduction to Law Studies*.[17] But in fact there are even older examples. The earliest such book is probably William Fulbeck's *Direction or Preparative to the Study of Law*,[18] published in 1599. But Fulbeck was not writing about the study of law at a university-affiliated law school or a faculty of law like those that operate today in Canada, the United States, and elsewhere. No such law schools

15 Glanville Williams, *Learning the Law* (London: Sweet & Maxwell, 1945). This popular book is now in its eighteenth edition. See Charlotte Harrison & Amanda Millmore, *Learning the Law* (London: Sweet & Maxwell, 2025).

16 Review of *Learning the Law*, (1945) 61:3 Law Q Rev 304 at 305.

17 Samuel Warren, *A Popular and Practical Introduction to Law Studies* (London: A Maxwell, 1835).

18 William Fulbeck, *Direction or Preparative to the Study of Law* (London: Thomas Wright, 1600).

existed in Fulbeck's time. He had in mind something very different. In the sixteenth century, young men[19] who wished to become barristers – the sort of lawyers who argued cases before the courts – studied with experienced barristers at the English Inns of Court. Fulbeck's book was aimed at preparing people for that sort of study.

TN: So, historically, English lawyers (at least "barristers," as we will discuss shortly) learned through apprenticeship at the Inns of Court. Did they not have to study any law at university at all?

CN: Lawyers, historically, at least in the English-speaking world, did not prepare for their vocation at universities. They might well have attended university before embarking on their professional careers to acquire a general liberal education. But not to study law. If this seems odd, consider, first, how the English universities once regarded – or one might say disregarded – the subject of law. Law – at least the English common law and its progeny – was not always considered a fit subject for university study. When law was studied at all in the ancient English universities (Oxford and Cambridge) prior to about the mid-eighteenth century, it was only civil law – that is, the law of the long-fallen ancient

19 Women were not permitted to become barristers in England until the passage of the *Sex Disqualification (Removal) Act* of 1919. The first woman to become a barrister in the UK was Ivy Williams, who was called to the bar in May 1922. That women were for so long unfairly prevented from being called to the bar for so long represents not only a disgraceful injustice to women but also a profound waste of talent that might have otherwise benefited English society as a whole. Things have changed significantly in the century since Ivy Williams was called to the bar. Today, female law students outnumber male students at most Canadian law schools, although there continue to be disappointing signs that women face challenges in the practice of law that lead them to leave the profession earlier and at higher rates than their male colleagues.

Roman Empire – or perhaps canon law, but not the law of England (or of Scotland or Wales, for that matter) – ancient or modern. There were lawyers in England, of course. But if they had attended university at all, they would have read (that is, majored or concentrated in) some academic subject other than law. Their trade they learned on the job, in the offices of experienced practitioners, or in one of the four London Inns of Court I have already mentioned to which all barristers were required to belong. The four Inns of Court – Lincoln's Inn, Gray's Inn, Inner Temple, and Middle Temple – are still very much in operation. They continue to play a distinguished role in the English legal profession. But over time the place of law at universities in the UK has changed markedly.

TN: *Why was English common law ignored for so long by English universities? It seems like a pretty strange oversight.*

CN: An intriguing answer to this question was offered by John Fortescue in his fifteenth-century work *De Laudibus Legum Angliae*[20] (often translated as "In Praise of English Laws"). Fortescue suggests that the universities' apparent disdain for the study of English law may have been related to language. Instruction in the great English universities was originally entirely in Latin. The laws of England, however, were embodied in various sources, only a few of which were written in Latin, while many others were written only in English or French. English law thus simply did not lend itself to study at the Latin-centric English universities.

20 John Fortescue, *Commendation on the Laws of England*, trans by Francis Grigor (London: Sweet & Maxwell, Ltd, 1917) at 80.

TN: *I know that law is studied at English universities today. And in the United States almost all American Bar Association accredited law schools are also affiliated with universities.*[21] *Here in Canada, too, law schools are not only university faculties but are also usually one of the most prestigious academic programs within those universities. So what changed? When did the law schools that we see today begin to take shape? Or what happened that at least started the ball rolling toward the direction of what law schools look like today?*

CN: A major breakthrough in English common law education occurred in 1758. In that year, a chair or professorship in English law was established for the first time at the University of Oxford. The holder of this chair had the title of "Vinerian Professor of Law" after its benefactor, Charles Viner. Viner had some years earlier produced his own massive 23-volume compilation of English law, titled *A General Abridgment of Law and Equity*.[22] That work had apparently made him quite a tidy sum of money and he was pleased to share his wealth (in his will) with Oxford.

The first holder of the Vinerian chair was William Blackstone. Blackstone, some years before this appointment, had begun to give a regular series of lectures on English law to Oxford students. These lectures were not part of the formal

21 There are a few notable exceptions, such as the New York Law School (not to be confused with NYU Law School), an independent law school that has been in operation for more than 125 years. See ABA, "List of ABA-Approved Law Schools," online: https://www.americanbar.org/groups/legal_education/resources/aba_approved_law_schools/in_alphabetical_order//.

22 Following Viner's death in 1756, bequests from his estate were used to create the Vinerian Chair. See David M Walker, *The Oxford Companion to Law* (Oxford: Clarendon Press, 1980) at 1277.

university curriculum. They were special "pay to attend" presentations. After his appointment to the Vinerian chair, Blackstone continued his regular lecture series on English law.

We know quite a bit about Blackstone's lectures, even including such little details as the cost of admission. The philosopher Jeremy Bentham – then still a teenager – came to hear Blackstone lecture and paid a fee of 6 guineas[23] to do so. (A guinea was worth £1, 1 shilling. So 6 guineas would be worth roughly £6.30, although the sum would not have been expressed that way at the time since this occurred many years – indeed centuries – before the decimalization of British currency in 1971.) Bentham was decidedly unimpressed by what he heard and later wrote a rather withering attack on Blackstone's reasoning in his essay entitled "A Fragment on Government."[24]

TN: It sounds like the lectures were unpopular then. I mean, I've definitely heard of Bentham, but not Blackstone.

CN: Bentham's name is certainly more widely remembered today, especially among people who have studied philosophy or perhaps economics. But among legal scholars, at least, William Blackstone is also something of a historical "rock star." And Bentham's critical view did not seem to reflect the popular opinion of Blackstone's lectures at all. They were very successful. And they apparently earned Blackstone rather a lot of money.

---

23 AV Dicey, "Blackstone's Commentaries" (1932) 4 Cambridge LJ 286 at 290.

24 J Bentham, "A Fragment on Government" in R Harrison, ed, *Bentham: A Fragment on Government* (Cambridge: Cambridge University Press, 1988). See also RA Posner, "Blackstone and Bentham" (1976) 19:3 JL & Econ 569.

Blackstone decided to publish an abridged version of his lectures in book form in 1756. This book, *An Analysis of the Laws of England,* was relatively short, but was an important forerunner to the magnum opus for which Blackstone would later become famous, around the world and for centuries to come, his *Commentaries on the Laws of England.*[25]

TN: So Blackstone helped popularize the university study of English law?

CN: After his appointment as the first holder of the Vinerian chair of English law at Oxford, Blackstone's lecture series evolved into the famous *Commentaries* mentioned above. But there is one particular part of those *Commentaries* that is especially noteworthy for people interested in the development of legal education.

The "Introduction" to the *Commentaries* consists of the first of the "Vinerian lectures." It was delivered by Blackstone on October 15, 1758. That first lecture was entitled "On the Study of Law."[26] Significantly, Blackstone was not referring in this introductory lecture to the study of law by those who intended to become practising lawyers. He was explaining why he considered the study of English common law at a university an important and worthy subject for all educated citizens. He did argue, though, that studying law could also be particularly useful for those who planned to practise law at some point in the future.

25 See William Blackstone, *Commentaries on the Laws of England,* edited by Stanley N Katz (Chicago: University of Chicago Press, 1979).

26 *Ibid,* Vol 1 at A2.

TN: It seems odd that that wouldn't already have been obvious to everyone. Why wouldn't studying law at university be widely accepted as not just important or "interesting" but essential for future lawyers?

CN: It does seem odd today that Blackstone was seen as a bit of a contrarian when he suggested that prospective lawyers might benefit from studying law at university, rather than pursuing other traditional undergraduate degree programs. But for many years there was no expectation, let alone any requirement, for those who wished to pursue the practice of law in England to study law at university.

TN: I'm trying to wrap my head around it all. So Blackstone thought university is where prospective lawyers – and other curious students, I assume – should learn about the law purely as an academic subject – in the way you would learn about history or philosophy. But he also thought it was the right place for them to learn law on their way to becoming practising lawyers? Was that what was considered a radical idea at the time?

CN: Well, it is important to appreciate what Blackstone thought the study of law at the university should entail and what it should not. He actually was not advocating for the university to become a place where aspiring lawyers would learn the basics of day-to-day legal practice. He was no proponent, in other words, of what fashionable educators today describe as "experiential learning." On the contrary. Blackstone saw that a university education in law (that is, English law, not Roman law) would greatly benefit legal practitioners precisely because such an education would *not* be concerned with the niceties of practice. He contrasted the proper role of legal education at the university with the traditional legal apprenticeship model in this way:

> [A] lawyer thus educated to the bar, in subservience to attorneys and solicitors, will find he has begun at the wrong end. If practice be the whole he is taught, practice must also be the whole he will ever know: if he is uninstructed in the elements and first principles upon which the rule of practice is founded, the least variation from established precedents will totally distract and bewilder him . . . he must never aspire to form, and seldom expect to comprehend, any arguments drawn *a priori,* from the spirit of the laws and the natural foundations of justice.[27]

It was long the case in the UK that it was possible to become a solicitor without studying law at university or, indeed, without completing a university degree at all,[28] although a new qualification system for solicitors introduced in 2021 will require those who wish to qualify as solicitors to complete the Solicitors Qualifying Examination, which will require a degree in some subject.[29]

TN: You have talked about "lawyers" in the UK. However, I know that in the UK there are two different types of lawyers: barristers (who argue in the higher courts), and solicitors (who perform other functions like drafting contracts, wills, and so on). You've

---

27 *Ibid* at 32.

28 See The Law Society, "Qualifying Without a Degree" (29 January 2025) online: https://www.lawsociety.org.uk/career-advice/becoming-a-solicitor/qualifying-without-a-degree.

29 Solicitors Regulation Authority, "Green Light for New Solicitor Exam," News Release (28 October 2020), online: https://www.sra.org.uk/sra/news/press/2020-press-release-archive/sqe-approved-lsb.

said that solicitors will require a university degree in some subject. What about barristers? Can barristers in England practise without a degree?

CN: We will have more to say about the distinction between "barristers" and "solicitors" in chapter 10. For now, we only need to note that the UK does have a so-called divided legal profession where some people choose to qualify as "barristers" while others qualify as "solicitors." In Canada, the two branches of the profession are merged, though in a number of formal and ceremonial ways the two distinct notional branches of the profession are preserved.

From as early as the late eighteenth century, when the Law Society of Upper Canada (now the Law Society of Ontario) was established, all qualified lawyers were entitled to practise as both barristers and solicitors,[30] a practice evidently borrowed from America.

Barristers in the UK are, in fact, required to have completed a university degree. Although that degree need not be in law, there is some practical benefit to studying law at university because prospective barristers who complete a degree in a non-law subject must also complete an additional course known as the Graduate Diploma in Law.[31] Significantly, however, it is apparently still the case that some eminent English lawyers and judges believe that aspiring

30 See Philip Girard, "The Making of the Canadian Legal Profession" (2014) 21:2 Int'l J Legal Prof 145 at 148.

31 Bar Standards Board, "Academic Component of Bar Training," online: https://www.barstandardsboard.org.uk/training-qualification/becoming-a-barrister/academic-component.html.

lawyers would actually be well advised to study something other than law at university.[32]

Law at UK universities, then, is not a professional degree program as it is in Canada and the United States. It continues to be an undergraduate degree program like history, philosophy, English literature, and so on. Students enter law degree programs directly after completing the British equivalent of secondary school. Although some British universities – including Oxford and Cambridge – have "Faculties of Law," these faculties are not quite like the second-entry law schools at US and Canadian universities to which only students who have already completed some years of university study may apply. Now, you might expect that, since law schools in UK universities are not professional programs that they are even more academic and theoretical than their US and Canadian counterparts. But this may not be the case at all. American legal scholar John Langbein, for example, argued in 1996 that

> the leading American law schools have transformed themselves into temples of scholarship, while English law schools have striven to become stronger as training centers for the profession . . . The contrast between English law schools as temples

32 Nicholas McBride, in a book written for aspiring British law students, has referred to the view that aspiring lawyers in the UK should study anything but law at university as "the astonishing hypothesis." He then proceeds to demonstrate why he rejects this hypothesis, though admitting that it is still a view held by many prominent members of the English legal profession, including a recently retired member of the UK Supreme Court. See Nicholas McBride, *Letters to a Law Student*, 5th ed (Harlow: Pearson Education Limited, 2022) at 45ff.

of scholarship and American law schools as training centers for the profession no longer bears the remotest relation to reality.[33]

TN: If the Canadian common law system derived from the UK, why is the law school system in Canada different?

CN: Although the Canadian and American common law systems both evolved from the English system, the study of law and the evolution of law schools in Canada and the United States followed a path that led to significant differences from the UK model. Modern Canadian common law schools were strongly influenced by developments in nineteenth-century American law school education. Lawyers in the United States, prior to the nineteenth century, learned their profession through apprenticeship. But some practitioners, not surprisingly, proved to be much better teachers and mentors than others. The most able of these lawyer-instructors were very much sought after by aspiring lawyers.[34] Some of these experienced lawyers began to attract so many prospective students that they found it worthwhile to operate small schools of law for them.

Some of these schools grew and attracted considerable renown. For example, two of the most well known were schools in Northampton, Massachusetts, and in Litchfield, Connecticut. The Northampton school apparently became an early source of faculty and students for the Harvard Law

33 John H Langbein, "Scholarly and Professional Objectives in Legal Education: American Trends and English Comparisons" in PBH Birks, ed, *What are Law Schools For? (Pressing Problems in the Law, Vol 2)* (Oxford: Oxford University Press, 1996) at 1, 3.

34 Louis D Brandeis, "The Harvard Law School" (1889) 1:1 Green Bag 10 at 11 ff.

School. The Litchfield school, founded by Tapping Reeve, was a particularly significant example of these early private or proprietary schools and, indeed, the Litchfield school was evidently the inspiration for another proprietary Connecticut law school, the New Haven Law School, which later became associated with Yale University and evolved into the Yale Law School.[35]

TN: *So these early schools were associated with practitioners, not with universities. Was that difference reflected in the teaching methods used? What would class look like in these old, small, private schools of law?*

CN: The teaching of law in these early law schools for apprentice-lawyers appears to have involved lecturing in the most literal sense: that is, instructors would read aloud to their students from their notes or perhaps from textbooks.[36] This method of law teaching was probably the dominant approach to teaching law in the United States – both in the proprietary law schools and the early university-affiliated law schools – until the mid-nineteenth century. There were some other features of the early law schools that have modern law school parallels. For example, it appears that moot courts – practice exercises in which students would argue mock appeal court cases – also formed part of the earliest

35 John H Langbein, "Blackstone, Litchfield and Yale: The Founding of Yale Law School" in AT Kronman, ed, *History of the Yale Law School* (New Haven: Yale University Press, 2008) 17; Yale Law School, "Origins of Yale Law School," online: https://law.yale.edu/about-yale-law-school/glance/our-history.

36 See, e.g., Eugene Wambaugh, "Professor Langdell – A View of His Career" (1906) 20:1 Harv L Rev 1.

law school programs. Writing about moot courts in 1868, Joel Prentiss Bishop claimed:

> §409. In law schools the practice acquired at moot courts is of considerable avail. This is an old method, always recommended, and adopted more or less by law students everywhere.[37]

Indeed, Bishop cites William Fulbeck's work that we mentioned earlier[38] in support of the view that moots had been an important part of legal education since at least the sixteenth century. Moots are still a distinctive part of Canadian law school education, and we will have more to say about them in chapter 9.

TN: *When did law school education start to migrate in North America from these private practitioner law schools to universities?*

CN: University-affiliated law schools began to appear in the United States in the late eighteenth and early nineteenth century, often competing head-to-head with the old proprietary law schools. It is usually thought that the oldest university law school in the United States is the William & Mary Law School, which dates its founding to 1779.[39] Sometimes it's difficult to pinpoint when law schools formally began because the official creation of a chair or professorship of law at a university might be regarded by that university as the beginning of a law school, even if there were no other

37 Joel Prentiss Bishop, *The First Book of the Law* (Boston: Little, Brown, and Company, 1868).

38 See above note 18.

39 See "About William & Mary Law School", online: https://law.wm.edu/about/.

faculty members or other institutional elements. Certainly, by the late nineteenth century there were law schools or law faculties at many American universities.

A major shift in North American legal education occurred in 1870 when Christopher Columbus Langdell was appointed the first dean of the Harvard Law School. Though Langdell was Harvard Law School's *first* dean, he was not the founding dean. The Harvard Law School had been in operation for over half a century before Langdell's appointment. But in its early years, it had not been organized like a modern university faculty. And faculty deans were, apparently, still a rather novel thing at Harvard in 1870.[40] Langdell's appointment was significant because Langdell came to Harvard with a specific vision for legal education. He considered law a science and conceived of legal education as a process by which students would discover the (relatively few) foundational principles upon which all of the common law rested. The Langdellian method of legal education, therefore, involved both an underlying theory of the nature of law and an approach to law teaching that emerged from that theory.

Langdell's pedagogical approach did not arise in a vacuum. Several years before Langdell arrived at Harvard, Theodore Dwight, the founding dean (or warden) of Columbia University's law school, had spearheaded a rather different attempt to regularize American university legal education, implementing the so-called Dwight Method,[41] a method

40 Charles W Eliot, "Langdell and the Law School" (1920) 33:4 Harv L Rev 518 at 519.
41 George Chase, "Dwight Method of Legal Instruction " (1894) 1 Cornell LJ 74.

of instruction emphasizing prior preparation by students and a classroom experience characterized by the professor's questions and the students' "recitations," rather than the lecture method that had previously characterized law schools.

TN: *You have talked about Langdell before. I know the Harvard Law School library is named after him, and I thought he was the inventor of the "case method" that we will look at more closely in chapter 6. But I have not heard of Theodore Dwight. What was the difference between Dwight's approach to legal education and Langdell's?*

CN: The Dwight Method and Langdell's method shared two common elements: an underlying belief that law was not simply a collection of arcane rules but was grounded in principles and could be studied on a scientific basis; and a de-emphasis on lecturing in favour of active student participation through the use of questions and answers (a method sometimes referred to as the "Socratic method"[42] because of its superficial similarity to the Socratic dialogues portrayed in the writings of Socrates' most famous pupil, Plato).

Where the two methods fundamentally differed was in the materials each professor used for the purpose of their classroom exercises. Dwight's method focused on the principles of law as found in published texts by learned

42 Dwight specifically described his approach as an example of the Socratic method. Theodore W Dwight, "Columbia College Law School, New York" (1889) 1:4 Green Bag 141 at 149.

authors,[43] rather than in the reasons for judgments (or opinions) issued by judges in previously decided cases.

In an 1894 article written by George Chase,[44] a former student and later colleague of Dwight's, the Dwight Method is explained in this way:

> [A]s the student is to meet the teacher in the classroom for only a limited portion of each day, it is important that he should come to receive the instruction with such a measure of preliminary knowledge of the subject to be considered as will enable him to understand the exposition and profit by it. For this purpose he should study carefully before each day's exercise so much of a valuable treatise upon the subject as will pertain to the special topic to be examined in the classroom on that particular day. Then in the classroom the teacher will, with plain direct questions, call upon him to recite and thus to exhibit what knowledge he has acquired of the topic and how well he has understood what he has studied. And so the teacher will pass from one to another of his class, asking each in turn to tell in his own words

43 *Ibid* at 145.

44 George Chase was one of the members of the Columbia University faculty who resigned in 1891 in protest over a decision by the president of Columbia College (the forerunner of today's Columbia University), Seth Low (himself a former student of Columbia's law school, according to Dwight [see above note 42 at 160]), to supplant the "Dwight Method" of teaching law at Columbia with Harvard's Langdellian case method. Following his departure from Columbia's law school, Chase became the founding dean of New York Law School. See James A Wooten, "Law School Rights: The Establishment of New York Law School, 1891–1897" (1991) 36 NYL Sch L Rev 337. New York Law School (not to be confused with New York University (NYU) Law School) continues to operate today as an independent, non-university-affiliated law school. It might be noted that shortly after he left Columbia, Chase was offered the deanship of the law school of the University of the City of New York (the university that became NYU in 1896), an offer he declined evidently because of his disappointing experience with the university bureaucracy he had experienced at Columbia. See Chase, above note 41.

> what he knows of the matter in hand, as point after point of the subject is developed. In this way the teacher will ascertain what his students do not know or have not understood, and will learn each one's special needs and the needs of the class as a whole. He should then on his own part meet and satisfy these special needs, by clear and easily-understood exposition, and by simple and interesting illustrations.[45]

Although this method – which emphasized student "recitations" over professorial lecturing – was considered novel for legal education, Dwight himself regarded it as no different from the method of instruction commonly used by American college professors in other disciplines at the time.[46] And to be sure, Dwight, like Langdell, also emphasized the notion that law ought to be regarded as a "science" rather than merely a "collection of 'modern instances'"[47] and described the method of teaching at Columbia as "the 'Socratic Method' of teaching."[48]

TN: So if Dwight was already using the "Socratic Method" at Columbia by the time Langdell arrived at Harvard, what was unique about the innovations introduced by Langdell at the Harvard Law School?

CN: First, Langdell's method was premised on a formalist perspective, emphasizing the notion that law could be

---

45 *Ibid* at 76.

46 Dwight, above note 42 at 146: "[I]t is worthy of remark that the methods pursued in the Columbia Law School closely connect themselves with collegiate training. Graduates of the Colleges find substantially the same methods of education in use here to which they have been already accustomed."

47 *Ibid* at 144.

48 *Ibid* at 150.

learned and understood entirely on its own terms – without the need to consider the insights or perspectives of other academic disciplines. Like the Dwight Method, Langdell's approach to teaching departed from the lecture method that had been the conventional mode of law school instruction, but Langdell's method differed from Dwight's in at least two respects. First, unlike Dwight, Langdell believed that the principles of law were best discovered by students through a careful consideration of the opinions (written judgments) of appeal court judges. Langdell believed, in other words, that law was best taught through inductive reasoning using as primary source material judgments of appellate courts. We'll explain in a little more detail what we mean by the inductive method in chapter 7. (Incidentally, some clue as to the origins of the case method are suggested by Joel Prentiss Bishop in *The First Book of the Law*.[49] Bishop notes that John William Smith in the early nineteenth century published a two-volume book containing 75 "leading cases," each of which was thought to establish a particular legal principle, with the author's notes on these cases. According to Bishop, this was "a new style of law book."[50]) A second distinguishing feature of the Langdell method is that the role of professorial exposition – lecturing or explaining by the professor – seemed to play a more limited role in Langdell's original classes. Toward the end of his career he did have to revert to lecturing, as we mention below.

49 Bishop, above note 37.
50 *Ibid* at §226.

Langdell's preferred method of instruction thus combined two approaches: the case method of study and the Socratic method of classroom instruction. Rather than focusing on the distillation of legal principles found in legal texts or treatises (which Dwight appeared to believe was of great importance, particularly for the majority of students of "average powers"[51]), Langdell used primary sources – the judicial decisions themselves – as material for his classes. And instead of imparting information by delivering lectures, he used a question-and-answer (recitation) method where the professor functioned more as an interlocutor of students than a dispenser of information.

TN: *Alright, but which is the better method: focusing on the textbook principles of law set down by experts or supposedly discovering legal principles for yourself from decided cases using an inductive method? (Like those physics experiments they made us do in high school to try to prove for ourselves how acceleration due to gravity works? I could never seem to get the same result twice.) So, give me the tea. Dwight or Langdell?*

CN: Because Dwight and Langdell were contemporaries, comparison of their respective methods was inevitable. Dwight maintained, among other things, that while he was not prepared to concede that Langdell's method was superior for any students, he was strongly of the view that it was decidedly inferior to Dwight's approach at least in the case of students of merely average ability.[52]

---

51 Dwight, above note 42 at 146ff.
52 *Ibid* at 146.

TN: Ok, spicy Dwight. But since Langdell seems to be much better known today, it seems that Langdell's method must have had a much greater long-term impact on legal education. So was Langdell's new approach to teaching law popular? Were students lining up to get into his classes?

CN: Langdell's approach was actually very unpopular during his first several years at Harvard. As one of Langdell's first students reports, "Attendance fell. Students wearied of the 'useless' preparation for the 'grammar school recitation' as it was called, and the number of those 'prepared' dwindled away to very few."[53] Students, alumni, and even members of the judiciary complained relentlessly, fearing that Langdell's ineffective method would ruin the Harvard Law School.[54] Indeed, Harvard's enrollment did fall significantly during the early years of Langdell's tenure.[55] But Harvard University president Charles Eliot stood by his appointee, resisting demands that he be dismissed. In the end, this proved to be a good decision. The Socratic/case method approach came to be closely associated with Langdell in particular and the Harvard Law School more generally and eventually proved to be the dominant form of instruction not only at Harvard but at law schools throughout the United States and in much of Canada as well.

TN: Many popular portrayals of American law schools – such as in the cinematic masterpiece Legally Blonde *– show law*

---

53 Franklin G Fessenden, "Rebirth of the Harvard Law School" (1919–1920) 33:4 Harv L Rev 493 at 500.

54 Samuel F Batchelder, "Christopher Columbus Langdell" (1906) 18:8 Green Bag 437 at 440.

55 Fessenden, above note 53 at 519–20.

professors using some kind of Socratic method. Is that what Canadian law students should expect also?

CN: We will return to this topic in chapter 6. There, we will see that although many Canadian law professors today might describe their teaching method as "Socratic," the modern version of the Socratic method is undoubtedly much gentler than the version that prevailed in earlier generations. It is also no longer the dominant approach to teaching law, especially in upper-year law courses. Some years ago it was suggested that even at Harvard the use of the Socratic method was on the decline.[56] But this "decline" appears to refer chiefly to the most unforgiving versions of the method, which could be seen as intimidating and almost bordering on a kind of institutionally sanctioned bullying. That version of the Socratic method has probably not been experienced by most law graduates for more than a generation.

TN: But apart from the methods of law school teaching, I'm still unclear about the content of law school teaching, especially the blend of practice and theory at Canadian law schools. For example, I know that not every law school class is even taught by a full-time university law professor. Many law school classes are taught by practising lawyers on a part-time or even volunteer basis. That makes sense to me. I assume those classes would be much more practical than courses taught by full-time professors who have never actually practised law. Once again, no offence, but wouldn't most students who plan to practise law prefer classes taught by practising lawyers?

---

56 Orin S Kerr, "The Decline of the Socratic Method at Harvard" (1999) 78 Nebraska L Rev.

CN: You are certainly right that many courses – especially specialized upper-year courses – are taught by distinguished experienced practitioners or sometimes judges. That is likely true at every law school in Canada. And law schools would not be able to offer the number or range of courses they do if it were not for the contribution of time and talent made by these part-time instructors. Those courses are, typically, much more practice-oriented, as you suggest. Some law students undoubtedly consider courses taught by experienced practitioners to be some of the most useful and enjoyable courses of their law school careers. But at the risk of being undiplomatic, not all practitioner-taught courses are viewed with equal fondness. Some of these courses, rightly or wrongly, are criticized for their lack of intellectual rigour. A commonly heard student complaint is that certain practitioner-taught courses consist principally of being endlessly regaled with "war stories" that are often entertaining but not always edifying. Some practitioners may also be disinclined to offer or encourage critical perspectives that challenge the status quo and help advance our understanding of the law. As a very prominent (finance) scholar once suggested to me, "Practitioners are very good at chopping trees. They are not always as good at figuring out which trees need to be chopped down."[57] As I'm sure you'll appreciate, that is certainly not true of all practitioners, of course.

57 The person who shared this observation with me was a scholar from another discipline. So he had never attended law school. He had, however, acquired considerable experience working with practitioners in another discipline and also had the distinction of having received a Nobel Prize.

From LL.B to JD

TN: Canadian law schools are an interesting combination of academic institutions and professional schools. To apply to law school you also have to have completed at least two years of university and, in most cases, law school applicants have completed at least one degree before starting law school. We saw in chapter 2 that the degree graduates of Canadian common law schools receive today is a "JD" or "Juris Doctor." But for some reason, this is not necessarily considered a true graduate degree. Why is that?

CN: Law in Canadian common law schools today is a "second-entry" program (in other words, you have to have already completed some university study before starting law school). But the JD degree – the degree you normally need to qualify to become a practising lawyer in Canadian common law jurisdictions – is only the first degree in law, not the highest university degree offered in law. It's true that before beginning a JD program a student is normally required to have completed at least some undergraduate university education, and the first law degree does include the word "doctor" in its title. But the JD is still generally considered an undergraduate degree, not an advanced degree. In fact, most Canadian law schools offer more advanced graduate degrees in law as well, including a Master of Laws (LLM) for which a JD is typically a prerequisite) and a doctoral-level degree designated at some law schools as a PhD in law and at other schools as an SJD (Doctor of Juridical Science). So, as you can see, despite the word "doctor" in the title of the degree, the JD degree is actually the lowest law degree in the Canadian academic pecking order.

The professional law degree did not always involve three years of full-time study and was not always designated as a "JD." When Langdell first came to Harvard, the degree taken by graduates of the Harvard Law School was the "Bachelor of Laws," or "LL.B" degree – the double "L" signifying the plural, "laws." This degree designation was, apparently, borrowed from the University of Cambridge,[58] though an almost identical designation ("Bachelor" or "Batchelor" of Law) had also been used for the first law degree granted by an American university, William & Mary University, in the late eighteenth century.[59]

Harvard's LL.B degree program, when Langdell was first appointed, involved less than two years of study and boasted no real academic standards. There were no examinations, for example, and the degree was essentially awarded to students who had attended classes for the required period – with proof of attendance, it seems, based largely on an honour system.[60] Langdell increased the time required to complete the degree to two full years and introduced examinations along with more rigorous academic standards. Later, evidently initially at the request of some students, an optional third year was added to the

58 The University of Cambridge began teaching English law in 1800 when the Downing Professorship of the Laws of England was established. Although the LL.B began as an undergraduate law degree, in 1922 only the BA was awarded to undergraduates studying law. The LL.B became, curiously, a de facto graduate degree. This situation continued until 1982, when the LLM replaced the LL.B. degree at Cambridge. See https://mcl.law.cam.ac.uk/why-the-mcl/the-faculty-of-law.

59 Alfred Zantzinger Reed, *Present-Day Law Schools in the United States and Canada* (Boston: Merrymount Press, 1928) at 77.

60 Fessenden, above note 53 at 494.

program.[61] That optional year later became mandatory, and the three-year LL.B degree soon became the standard not only at Harvard but at other schools throughout the United States as well.

When the first university-affiliated common law school in Canada was established at Dalhousie University in 1883, it adopted the model of the three-year LL.B degree program. Eventually, this model became the norm throughout the common law provinces, although the acceptance of the proposition that three years of full-time university academic study was the appropriate way to prepare for a legal career took some time to be accepted, particularly in Ontario.

In the meantime, beginning in the early twentieth century, many voices called for the designation of US law degrees to be upgraded and standardized. So, for example, a number of US law schools – most notably the University of Chicago, Stanford, and the University of California – began offering a JD degree instead of an LL.B to their graduates, all of whom had been required to complete a college degree before their admission to law school.[62] The Harvard Law School, which also had adopted a requirement for incoming law students to have first completed a college degree, petitioned the university in 1902 to allow it to offer a JD degree as well.[63] This petition was denied, however, and it was not until 1969 that the Harvard Law School first offered

---

61 *Ibid* at 509.

62 James Parker Hall, "American Law School Degrees" (1907) 6:2 Mich Law Rev 112 at 114. Stanford apparently reverted to the LL.B degree in 1927. See David Perry, "How Did Lawyers Become Doctors? From the LL.B. to the J.D." (2012) 84 NY St BJ at 28.

63 Hall, *ibid* at 113.

a JD degree.[64] The JD designation – thought to be the legal equivalent of medical schools' MD degree – was apparently adopted from a German university law degree, the *Juris Utriesque Doctor.*[65] Adopting the obvious alternative degree designation – Doctor of Laws (LL.D) – was not feasible since that degree, in the United States, had already become (and remains today) a conventional honorary degree bestowed by universities as an honorific title on distinguished convocation speakers, rather than an earned degree.[66] At some law schools, the JD degree was reserved for those law graduates who had completed another undergraduate degree before entering law school, while the LL.B degree was awarded to students for whom it was their first degree.[67] The JD degree was also used at some American schools to denote particular academic distinction – rather as universities today award degrees "with distinction" or "*cum laude.*"[68]

Early in the twentieth century, calls began in the United States for law schools offering their graduates LL.Bs to rename the LL.B degree to the JD, to better reflect the

64 David N Hollander, "Law Faculty Approves Awarding J.D. Degree in Place of the LL.B.," *The Harvard Crimson* (March 12, 1969), online: https://www.thecrimson.com/article/1969/3/12/law-faculty-approves-awarding-jd-degree.

65 Zantzinger Reed, *Present Day Law Schools in the United States and Canada* at 78–79.

66 *Ibid* at 78.

67 While Canadian LL.B programs did typically require incoming students to have completed at least two years of university study before entering law school, they did not require applicants for admission to have first completed an undergraduate degree. At one time, many Canadian university degree programs could be completed in three years, so it is probable that many students chose to complete an undergraduate degree before attending law school despite the fact that they were not required to do so.

68 Perry, above note 62 at 28.

advanced, professional nature of a law degree program.[69] However, the major turning point in the US LL.B./JD debate came in 1964 when the Section of Legal Education and Admissions to the Bar of the American Bar Association recommended for all approved American law schools "favorable consideration of the conferring of the degree of Juris Doctor (JD) by such schools on those students who successfully complete the program leading to the first professional degree in law."[70] This watershed event signalled the beginning of what would eventually become a universal adoption by American universities of the JD designation, although, it should be said, the sweeping change was gradual, not immediate. Some schools – including, most notably, the Yale Law School – continued to resist calls to relabel their LL.B degree as a JD. However, the trend became unstoppable. Even Yale eventually capitulated and, since 1971, has offered the JD degree.[71]

In Canada, the adoption of the JD degree was a much more recent phenomenon. Canadian common law schools, beginning with the Dalhousie Law School, had offered the LL.B degree since the late nineteenth century. It was not until the turn of the twenty-first century that the University of Toronto Faculty of Law first decided to change the name of its professional law degree from LL.B to JD in 2001. Various explanations, both official and rumoured, were offered

---

69 See, e.g., (1904) 18 Harvard Law Review 51.

70 See John G Hervey, "Time for a Change from LL.B. to J.D. Degree" (1965) 10:5 Student LJ 5.

71 Yale Law School, "The Modern Law School: 1955–1979," online: https://library.law.yale.edu/modern-law-school-1955-1979.

for this change. For example, it was suggested that the LL.B degree misleadingly suggested that law was a first-entry degree program, like a typical BA degree.Yet all LL.B students were required to have first completed at least two years of pre-law university study and, as a practical matter, most students came to law school after having completed an undergraduate degree. There was an additional consideration. An increasing number of Canadian law school graduates were seeking employment at US firms, especially in New York City. Changing the designation of the first degree in law from LL.B to JD signalled that the Canadian three-year law degree was comparable to the US JD degree. There had even been suggestions that such a change was needed to prevent salary discrimination by US employers against LL.B holders.[72]

At first, many other Canadian law schools staunchly resisted the change. To many Canadian law faculty members and not a few of their alumni, such a proposal seemed, among other things, an unnecessary affront to Canadian legal academic traditions, an unwarranted Americanization of Canadian legal education, and even a cynical attempt to appease the relatively small number of American employers of recent Canadian law school graduates. But gradually all Canadian common law schools adopted the new designation – most even deciding to offer to all prior graduates the opportunity to exchange their LL.Bs for JDs if they wished. So it is that many senior practising lawyers in Canada today

72 "A Rose by Any Other Name," *Canadian Lawyer* (March 17, 2008).

now boast JD degrees, even if no such degree was actually offered by their law school at the time they graduated.

Conclusion

The relationship between the modern university-affiliated law school and the practice of law is a complicated one.[73] Law students may be understandably confused about how law schools view their own mission and the role of their students and faculty members. In the next chapter we will look into this question more closely as we examine the design and educational goals of the typical Canadian law school curriculum.

73 For an especially lucid and frequently cited discussion of the issue of practical lawyer education versus academic legal education, see William Twining, "Pericles and the Plumber" in William Twining, ed, *Law in Context: Enlarging a Discipline* (Oxford: Oxford University Press, 1997) at 63.

5

the curriculum basics

What's So Special about Law School?

Law school is distinct from most undergraduate university degree programs in at least one major way: It is both a university program within a university faculty and also a professional program that is subject to professional recognition or accreditation standards. But is law school really much different from any other university program? After all, many university programs have high admissions standards, are very challenging, and require students to develop excellent reasoning and writing skills. So why do first-year law students often complain that studying law is much more demanding than anything they have studied before? What's so special about law school?

To try to answer that question, we want to look at three things: the content of law school courses (the topic of this chapter), the method of teaching (chapter 6), and the methods of evaluation at law schools (chapter 8).

Let's start by looking at the content of law school courses. We are going to focus in particular on the first year of law school because, at most Canadian law schools, all or most of the first-year courses are mandatory, while most second- and third-year courses are elective. So after the first year, students can for the most part design their program around their own particular interests. It is only in the first year that students share a fairly similar experience.

The Canadian Common Law School Curriculum

TN: *Since most first-year courses are mandatory, and common law schools are all subject to the same Federation of Law Societies National Requirement (that we will talk about in a moment), we might expect that the first-year program would be more or less the same at every law school. But there are differences. We've produced a table in Appendix B at the end of this chapter that maps out the first-year courses at each Canadian English-language common law school. There are obvious similarities, but there are significant differences too. Is there a goal or theme that is common to all first-year law school programs in Canada?*

CN: The main goal of the first year is to introduce students to the foundational principles and concepts of law and some of the most important building blocks of the common law system. Each law school has its own distinct vision as to how best to do that. But I think we can fairly say that, although the various programs are not all identical, they have far more similarities than differences.

For example, the first-year (or "1L")[1] program at most Canadian common law schools includes courses in torts, contracts, criminal law, property, and legal research and writing. Many also include courses in constitutional law, legal ethics or professionalism, Aboriginal law and Indigenous law, and a foundations or orientation to law course. Most of those courses will be taken by students at every law school before they graduate, but some schools offer them in the upper years rather than in first year.

The general similarity of first-year course offerings at Canadian law schools, though, is unmistakable. Incidentally, the same basic slate of courses – including, especially, contracts, torts, criminal law, constitutional law, and property law – is typically part of the first-year curriculum at US law schools as well.

TN: *Have these "standard" courses always been mandatory for first-year law students in Canada?*

CN: What might be described as a sort of "standard" Canadian/US law school curriculum – especially a first-year curriculum – does seem to be very old. In an article on the

1 Referring to first year law students as "1Ls" (and upper year students as "2Ls" and "3Ls") was originally regarded in Canada exclusively as an American practice, though the terms were well known in Canada for many years owing perhaps, among other things, to the popularity among law students of Scott Turow's 1977 best-selling account of his first year at the Harvard Law School, *One-L: The Turbulent True Story of a First Year at Harvard Law School* (New York: Putnam, 1977). It is not clear when use of this American term migrated across the border and entered the Canadian law student lexicon but casual observation suggests this probably began to occur sometime in the early twenty-first century, perhaps around the same time that Canadian law schools began offering the JD degree.

Harvard Law School written more than 130 years ago,[2] Louis Brandeis, who eventually was appointed to the US Supreme Court, recorded the course of study at the Harvard Law School for the year 1888–89. The first-year list of courses consisted of contracts, torts, property, criminal law, and civil procedure. With the notable exception of constitutional law, which in 1888 was a third-year course at the Harvard Law School, you can see that Harvard's nineteenth-century first-year curriculum has much in common with the typical twenty-first-century first-year program at Canadian law schools, as you have set out in Appendix B.

TN: *When you see that law school programs – at least first-year programs – haven't changed radically since back in the days when people were travelling by horse and buggy and using slide rules and abacuses to do calculations, it raises a few questions. Does this mean that law school programs had already been basically perfected by the late 1800s, so that only the most minor revisions since that time have been considered necessary? Or is there a more troubling answer? Are law schools simply overly conservative and now find themselves hopelessly stuck in the past and insufficiently attuned to the social and technological changes that have occurred over the past 150 years?*

CN: Reasonable people may well differ about whether the standard first-year law school curriculum is the product of blinkered conservative thinking or a wise reflection of the old maxim "If it ain't broke, don't fix it." But it is probably no real surprise that the programs of Canada's common law

2 Louis D Brandeis, "The Harvard Law School" (1889) 1:1 Green Bag 10.

schools are so similar. And while the explanation might well be linked to some kind of institutional conservatism, it isn't necessarily a matter of *academic* conservatism.

All common law schools must satisfy the National Requirement prescribed by the Federation of Law Societies of Canada (FLSC) to entitle their graduates to be eligible to enter a bar admission program in any of Canada's common law provinces. The FLSC describes itself as "the national association of the 14 law societies mandated by the provinces and territories to regulate Canada's legal profession in the public interest."[3] The FLSC's National Requirement[4] sets out the requirements that applicants to a Canadian bar admission program in any common law province must satisfy. Those requirements include "completion of an LL.B or JD degree that has been accepted by the [FLSC]."[5] Acceptance (or approval) of a Canadian common law degree program requires a law school to satisfy certain criteria that include offering a program that will prepare students to satisfy the "competency requirements" in certain areas that the FLSC considers necessary for entry into a Canadian bar admission program. So to that extent, there is, at

3 See Federation of Law Societies of Canada home page, online: https://flsc.ca.

4 FLSC, "National Requirement (January 1, 2018)," online: https://flsc.ca/wp-content/uploads/2024/04/National-Requirement-Jan-2018.pdf [National Requirement]. A new version of the National Requirement will take effect January 1, 2029. Because the new National Requirement will apply to all law school graduates who graduate beginning in 2029, the new requirement will effectively apply to common law school programs when students who expect to graduate in 2029 begin their three-year law degree – that is, from September 2026. See FLSC, "National Requirement (In Effect January 1, 2029)," online: https://flsc.ca/wp-content/uploads/2024/04/NRR-approved-on-March-12-2024-ENG.pdf.

5 National Requirement, *ibid.*

least unofficially and indirectly, a sort of a core set of course requirements that every common law school must offer.

TN: The idea of a "national requirement" is interesting because my understanding is that lawyers are regulated on a province-by-province basis. When a person gets called to the bar, they are called to the bar of one particular province only. So what exactly is the basis for the FLSC's authority to set out a "national requirement" for Canadian law schools?

CN: As you point out, every province and territory has its own law society or barristers society that has the responsibility of regulating the legal profession. One of the most important aspects of that responsibility is determining who is admitted to practice and overseeing and disciplining lawyers. (The profession in Quebec is organized a little differently, and so there are two separate regulators in Quebec. But most of our focus will be on Canada's common law jurisdictions.)

The first version of the FLSC's National Requirement was established in 2009. The current version of the National Requirement was approved on March 12, 2024, and will be in effect for students graduating after January 1, 2029 – in other words, for students who begin a three-year JD program any time after September 2026.

The National Requirement came about as a result of a number of developments in the last 15 or 20 years. As we saw in chapter 4, we haven't always had university-affiliated law schools in Canada. In Ontario in particular, leaving aside a few "false starts" in the late nineteenth century, there were no university-affiliated law schools until 1947, when the University of Toronto Faculty of Law, in its modern form, opened its doors. But the launch of the modern University of Toronto Faculty of Law – and in particular the move to U of T of key Osgoode Hall faculty members in 1949 – was the culmination of a fierce dispute about the proper approach to legal education. On one side of the dispute were some prominent leaders in Ontario legal education (including one future chief justice of the Supreme Court of Canada). On the other side was the Law Society of Upper Canada (as the Law Society of Ontario was then known).

The dispute centred on the goal and structure of legal education. In Ontario prior to 1947, there was only one law school in Ontario: Osgoode Hall Law School, which was then operated by the Law Society itself from its headquarters on Queen Street in Toronto, many years before the modern Osgoode Hall became a faculty of York University. The program at Osgoode Hall was a three-year program, but it did not consist of three years of full-time academic work. Students would attend lectures for about two hours each day, then spend the rest of their time working essentially as legal apprentices in lawyers' offices. It was the quintessential "experiential education." But for Osgoode law professors who had been to Harvard (such as Cecil (Cesar) Wright and Bora Laskin), it was obvious that this practice-focused legal education was a very pale and inferior version of the programs offered by first-rate university-affiliated law schools in the United States, such as Harvard Law School.

In response to the urgings of the very small handful of professors at Osgoode Hall and, evidently, students as well, the Law Society of Upper Canada struck a committee in

1946 to investigate legal education in Ontario. The committee issued its recommendations in 1949, rejecting, among other things, the suggestion that Ontario should adopt a model of legal education involving three years of full-time academic study in place of Osgoode Hall's lecture/law office model. Cecil Wright and Bora Laskin, then faculty members at Osgoode Hall who had strongly supported the call for full-time legal education, promptly resigned from Osgoode Hall following the release of the committee's recommendations. As Bora Laskin would later explain, he and Wright believed they had no choice but to resign given that the report not only rejected the idea of a full-time law school, but also was harshly critical of the "attitudes" of those members of the Osgoode Hall faculty who had publicly expressed their disapproval of the existing "concurrent system of training and a full-time Law School."[6]

Laskin's frustration with both the tone and content of the committee's report is revealed in a comment he made in a lecture at the University of Toronto in 1982 in honour of Cecil Wright:

> Let me turn to other parts of the report, which was unbelievable in its obtuseness and in its smugness. It would be laughed at as some joke in 1982; it was equally a joke in 1949 . . .[7]

Following their resignation from Osgoode Hall, both Wright and Laskin went in 1949 to the recently established

6 Bora Laskin, "Cecil A Wright: A Personal Memoir" (1983) 33:2 U Toronto LJ 148 at 155, citing a passage from the so-called Cartwright Report.

7 *Ibid* at 158.

Faculty of Law at the University of Toronto. However, for almost a decade, the Law Society of Upper Canada refused to accept the University of Toronto's three-year LL.B program as fully equal to the Law Society's own three-year Osgoode Hall program. Thus, any aspiring lawyer who chose to study law at the University of Toronto Faculty of Law would, upon graduation, be required to spend one additional year at Osgoode Hall, presumably to bring their legal training up to the standard required of an Ontario lawyer.

This arrangement finally ended in 1957 when the Law Society agreed to recognize full-time, three-year law degree programs at university-affiliated law schools as equivalent to an Osgoode Hall education. It was this change that led to the founding of law schools at several other universities in Ontario. A few years later, Osgoode Hall Law School itself left the Law Society and moved to York University, where it continues to this day.[8]

TN: Does that mean that, at least in Ontario, prior to 1947, when there were no university law schools, if you wanted to become a lawyer the only show in town was Osgoode Hall Law School, which was not part of any university but was run by the Law Society itself? That almost sounds a bit like the old

8 The story of the battle that led to the modern structure of Ontario legal education is a fascinating one of which there are many excellent accounts. In addition to the first-person recollections of Bora Laskin referred to above, for example, Cecil Wright also set down his version of the events in Cecil A Wright, "Should the Profession Control Legal Education? (The Law Society of Upper Canada: A Professional Monopoly)" (1950) 3:1 J Legal Educ 1. Wright also offered his reflections on the role and purpose of legal education in Cecil A Wright, "The University Law Schools " (1950) 28:2 Can B Rev 140.

eighteenth-century proprietary law schools in the United States that were described in chapter 4.

CN: It's true that there were no long-lasting university law programs before 1947, although there had been much earlier unsuccessful attempts to launch such programs at the University of Western Ontario, Queen's University, and the University of Toronto. Before 1957, any Ontario university could, of course, have chosen to offer a degree program in law. It's just that those programs would not have had any formal approval or accreditation from any body governing the legal profession. So they wouldn't offer a gateway into the legal profession, and that seemed to be the weakness that prevented the pre-1947 initiatives at various Ontario universities from thriving.

And of course, it's still the case that universities can offer degree programs in law that are entirely academic in nature. As we discussed in chapter 4, universities in the United Kingdom, for example, have done just this for many years. And some Canadian universities today offer undergraduate degrees in law (or in legal studies) that do not qualify their graduates to seek entry into the legal profession. Carleton University in Ottawa, for example, has for many years offered a BA degree in law through its Department of Law and Legal Studies, which is not intended to, and does not, make graduates eligible to seek admission to bar admission programs. Programs like this must satisfy the academic quality standards of any other university undergraduate degree program, but they do not need to meet any other requirements prescribed by bodies outside the university governing the legal profession.

TN: The FLSC didn't establish its first National Requirement for common law students until 2009. But Canadian law schools had been around for decades before that. They must have been subject to some kind of professional accreditation or approval standards before 2009. What were the standards a university law school had to meet prior to 2009 to entitle its graduates to apply for admission to the bar in a Canadian province or territory?

CN: There were earlier professional approval initiatives, but they were not national in scope and they weren't always vigorously enforced or dutifully observed. Today, if a Canadian university wishes to offer a degree program that entitles its graduates to seek admission to the bar and so eventually become a lawyer, it must ensure its program satisfies the requirements established by the relevant provincial law societies or barristers society for that purpose. That's what the National Requirement is all about. I'll return to the National Requirement in a moment. The fact that law schools are university faculties but must still satisfy external professional accrediting bodies has led to occasional tensions between law school faculties and the legal profession over the years.

The regulation of the legal profession in Canada is a provincial rather than a federal matter; so each province has its own law society or barristers society. Individual provincial law societies had promulgated their own policies relating to law school programs in their respective provinces in years past – sometimes in the fairly distant past. In Ontario, for example, the Law Society of Upper Canada (as it was then called) originally required in 1957 that all approved law schools offer 25 specified courses. Eleven of those 25 courses were to be mandatory for all students. (In 1969, the Law Society reduced the number of mandatory courses from 11 to 7.)

TN: This next question seems obvious. What were the original mandatory courses? Should we think of those courses as the most important, core law school courses, at least for students who intend to go on to practice law?

CN: The Law Society's original 11 mandatory law school courses were as follows:

- Agency
- Evidence
- Company law (corporate law)
- Wills
- Constitutional law of Canada
- Civil procedure
- Contracts
- Criminal law and procedure
- Personal property
- Real property
- Torts

Whether these courses ever were (or should now be) regarded as the most fundamental law school courses is, needless to say, something about which reasonable people might differ.

TN: When the list of mandatory courses was lowered from 11 to 7, which four courses were removed from this list? Had something happened within the profession or in society that had convinced the Law Society that those four courses just weren't as important any longer?

CN: The first four courses on the above list were deleted from the mandatory course list when it was revised in 1969:[9] agency, evidence, company law, and wills. I frankly don't know what the specific rationale was either for including those courses originally or for deciding to drop them from the list of mandatory courses in 1969. Although the seven remaining courses might for some time thereafter have technically been considered "core courses" for an approved law school curriculum, it is frankly unlikely that most Canadian law professors (or most Canadian practising lawyers, for that matter) were even aware of the Law Society's formal law school curriculum mandate. In fact, although all of the seven mandatory courses from 1969 still play a significant role in the curricula of Canadian common law schools, the same cannot be said for all of the 25 courses that the Law Society originally regarded as apparently so important that every approved law school was required at least to offer them (although law students could freely choose whether or not to take any of them). It is somewhat telling that several of those 25 courses are no longer taught regularly (or even at all) at many Canadian law schools.[10]

TN: Were all of these "mandates" imposed to help students eventually pass their bar examinations and be called to the bar? How strongly did the provincial law societies police law school

9 The Law Society of Upper Canada's 1969 law course requirements are reproduced as an appendix to the FLSC's Task Force on the Canadian Common Law Degree, "Final Report" (October 2009), online (pdf): https://www.slaw.ca/wp-content/uploads/2009/10/Task-Force-Final-Report.pdf.

10 Such courses would include, for example, agency, banking and bills of exchange, equity, and sale of goods. Sale of goods is often, though not invariably, included in courses on "Commercial Law."

programs to ensure they were preparing law students sufficiently to pass their exams and, eventually, to become competent to practise law?

CN: Beyond periodic grumblings among some members of the profession that law schools were hopelessly theoretical and insufficiently practical, for many years following the promulgation of the Law Society's 1969 law faculty approval requirements, the prevailing attitude of the bar toward Canadian legal education seems to have largely been one of benign neglect. The situation changed in the twenty-first century when the Federation of Law Societies of Canada – the body to which the provincial and territorial lawyers' governing bodies belonged – appointed a task force to review academic requirements for bar admission nationally.

TN: What change occurred in the twenty-first century that suddenly led to this task force being created? Were law school graduates failing bar admission examinations in greater numbers? Was there some public outcry about the declining competency of Canadian lawyers?

CN: Well, several factors led to the creation of this task force. First, several Canadian provinces had introduced legislation intended to ensure the transparency, objectivity, impartiality, and fairness of admission requirements to *all* regulated professions, including the legal profession.[11] Second, there had been an increasing number of applicants to Canadian

11 See, e.g., *Fair Access to Regulated Professions and Compulsory Trades Act, 2006* (Ontario), SO 2006, c 31; *Fair Registration in Regulated Professions Act* (Manitoba), CCSM c F12; *Fair Registration Act* (Nova Scotia), SNS 2008, c 38. (Several other provinces also adopted similar legislation somewhat later.)

bar admission programs who had obtained their legal education at institutions outside Canada. In order to assess fairly what educational requirements should be expected of these foreign-trained bar admission applicants, it was recognized that there needed to be some more formalized standards for Canadian common law education in general.

TN: Why would that be necessary? Wouldn't it have made more sense to deal with assessing the qualifications of foreign-trained applicants on a one-by-one basis? It seems unlikely that, among the number of immigrants to Canada each year, a significant number of them would be foreign-trained lawyers.

CN: In the past, most foreign-trained applicants for admission to the bar were indeed newcomers to Canada. But an important new phenomenon was emerging. Universities, particularly in Australia and the United Kingdom, were actively advertising undergraduate law programs to attract Canadian students interested in studying law.[12] Many of these programs even included courses in Canadian law often taught by Canadian law professors. In fact, an increasing number of Canadian students were choosing to study law at these universities outside Canada rather than at Canadian law schools, with a view to subsequently seeking to return to Canada to practise law.[13] Canadian law societies had

---

12 See, e.g., Bond University, "Study Canadian Law," online: https://bond.edu.au/bond-canadian-law-program; University of Birmingham, "Canadian Students at Birmingham Law School," online: https://www.birmingham.ac.uk/schools/law/courses/international/canada.

13 A report for the Law Society of Ontario in 2016 stated that of the 2,350 new candidates to become licensed as lawyers in Ontario, about 600 were candidates who had received their legal education outside Canada, of which some 35 percent were Canadian-born candidates who had gone abroad for their legal education and

established a process for reviewing and accrediting foreign law degree programs undertaken by applicants from abroad seeking to become qualified to practise law in Canada. But the number of applicants was now very large, including this significant number of Canadians who had chosen to study law abroad. In order to fairly determine what would constitute the foreign equivalent to an approved Canadian law school education, it became important to define more clearly the essential requirements of such programs for both foreign and domestic institutions.

TN: Why did so many universities in Australia and the UK start actively pursuing Canadian students to study law there?

CN: Presumably, these universities began to recognize that there was a significant latent demand in Canada for legal education that wasn't being satisfied by the relatively small number of Canadian law schools. Some commentators have suggested that the number of places available in Canadian law schools had not kept pace with the growth of the Canadian population and the Canadian economy. Needless to say, this is a very sensitive issue. Many practising lawyers were strongly opposed to significant expansion of Canadian law schools because of the impact that expansion might have on the economics of the Canadian legal profession. The mandatory "articling" requirement, a kind of legal apprenticeship that we will

were now returning to Canada to seek admission to the bar. See Law Society of Upper Canada, Professional Development and Competence Committee, "Report to Convocation" (22 September 2016) at 13, online (pdf): https://www.advocates.ca/Common/Uploaded%20files/Advocacy/Submissions/LawSocietyofUpperCanada/LSUC_PDC_Committee_Report.pdf.

discuss in a little more detail in chapter 10, was already under significant pressure, at least in Ontario. Not all law school graduates were able to obtain "articling" positions after law school. And successfully completing articles of clerkship was a requirement for admission to the bar. The shortage of articling positions (the "articling crisis," as it came to be known) led to the creation of an alternative path to bar admission that we will also discuss in greater detail in chapter 10.

The key point is that Canadian law schools simply did not expand to meet the growing demand for law school places. Foreign universities in jurisdictions with similar common law systems – the UK and Australia – recognized that many Canadian students would be more than willing to attend (and pay tuition to) law schools there, provided that the degrees they earned would eventually enable them to become qualified to practise in Canada. There could also be certain other advantages to studying law abroad. Because law is an undergraduate degree program in the UK, for example, a Canadian student could potentially finish their law school education more quickly there. And, of course, there were a number of intangible benefits. Many of the universities interested in attracting Canadian students were in pleasant locations and offered students wonderful travel opportunities while they pursued their legal studies.

TN: So the increasing number of Canadian bar admission applicants who had been educated abroad was one key factor in the FLSC's decision to become more proactive in setting uniform standards for legal education. Were there other changes that prompted the task force to become more "hands on" in 2009?

CN: A third important consideration came from the proliferation of new Canadian law schools. After the initial flurry of new university-affiliated law schools that had opened shortly after the decision by Ontario's Law Society in 1957 to fully approve university law school programs on the same basis as that of the Law Society's own law school, the Canadian law school environment had remained relatively stable for decades. Then, beginning in the early 2000s, there were a number of proposals advanced for the creation of new Canadian law schools. Not all of the law schools proposed by universities at that time materialized. But several did, including Thompson Rivers University Faculty of Law, Bora Laskin Faculty of Law at Lakehead University, and the law school known today as the Lincoln Alexander School of Law at Toronto Metropolitan University. In order for provincial law societies to be able to determine on a fair, credible, and reasonable basis whether to approve the proposed programs at these new law schools for accreditation purposes, it was important to establish clear, transparent criteria that would apply equitably to the graduates of all accredited or approved law schools.

TN: It's interesting that this push for accreditation occurred at a national level even though the legal profession in each province – including entry into the legal profession – is controlled by a provincial law society in that province.

CN: There were compelling reasons for provincial and territorial law societies to work together to establish a national framework for law school accreditation.

As the 2009 report of the FLSC's Task Force on the Canadian Common Law Degree noted, the federal government and Canadian provincial governments sought greater labour mobility for members of all regulated professions, including the law profession. In particular, the "Labour Mobility" provisions of the Agreement on Internal Trade[14] entered into between the federal government and the governments of every Canadian province and territory provides that, with limited exceptions, "any worker certified for an occupation by a regulatory authority of [any province or territory] shall, upon application, be certified for that occupation by each other [province or territory] which regulates that occupation" without imposing material additional requirements.[15]

TN: *Every Canadian law school is a university faculty. I assume that means they are not under any obligation to comply with curriculum requirements imposed by organizations outside the university, like the FLSC or provincial law societies. But presumably if a law school isn't officially "approved" or "accredited," students wouldn't be as willing to attend and pay tuition, either. So the task force could not actually require law schools to follow its recommendations, but would reasonably expect that they all would. What was the task force's overall effect on Canadian law schools?*

CN: The 2009 task force report eventually led to the adoption by the FLSC of a "national requirement" for Canadian common law schools. The FLSC's National Requirement sets out the requirements that applicants to a Canadian

14 Online: https://www.cfta-alec.ca/wp-content/uploads/2024/04/Consolidated-with-14th-Protocol-final-draft.pdf.

15 *Ibid*, s 706.

bar admission program in any common law province must satisfy. Students who have completed their law school education in Canada must have completed a JD or LL.B degree that has been "accepted" by the FLSC. A JD or LL.B degree will be "accepted" by the FLSC if the program leading to the degree satisfies a number of criteria relating to such things as the adequacy of the law school's resources and the sufficiency of the number of credits and ensures that the holders of the degree have met the "competency requirements" described in the National Requirement. Those "competency requirements" include a number of "skills requirements" dealing with things like legal research, problem solving, and oral and written legal communication. They also include requirements relating to knowledge and skills pertaining to legal ethics and professionalism and demonstrated understanding of matters relating to truth and reconciliation.

TN: Do law students have to take any steps on their own to be sure they have met the "competency requirements" that entitle them to be admitted to a provincial bar admission program? Or is it sufficient to attend and graduate from an "approved" Canadian common law school?

CN: Basically, graduating from an approved law school will mean that a law student will have satisfied the appropriate requirements. All of the requirements are reflected in various aspects of Canadian law school programs in addition to requirements relating to "substantive legal knowledge" that reflect a view of the "core" components of a common law degree that has persisted for more than 150 years.

TN: So the National Requirement should give us a good general introduction to some of the most basic elements of a Canadian common law degree program. I've looked at the National Requirement. It includes a number of specific topics, but it doesn't always include detailed information about what law school courses on those various topics should include. For example, the National Requirement calls for bar admission applicants to have demonstrated an understanding of

- *the "foundations of law," and*
- *the principles of private law, public law, and Indigenous law.*

How do these requirements get translated into a law school curriculum?

CN: Each of these items is complex and challenging. They all merit close, careful, and lengthy study. We will offer only a few introductory and unforgivably superficial observations about them here.

Foundations of Law

The "foundations of law" of which the FLSC expects aspiring lawyers to demonstrate understanding must include four components:

1. Principles of common law and equity
2. Sources and authorities of Indigenous law
3. The process of statutory construction and analysis
4. The administration of law in Canada[16]

16 National Requirement, above note 4.

Common Law and Equity

TN: Alright, I'll ask: What is the distinction between "common law" and "equity"? I think of equity basically as fairness. Shouldn't the common law always be aimed at fairness?

CN: The distinction between "common law" and "equity" in the common law world has a technical meaning. Let's start with common law. The *Oxford Companion to Law* suggests that the term "common law" is used in at least seven different senses.[17] In its most basic sense, though, the "common law" was the law common to all of England, rather than any distinct regional laws or customs. The term is also used to distinguish the English system of laws from those of civil law systems (where the law is codified rather than evolved through decisions of the courts) and to distinguish the somewhat rigid system of rules developed by the common law courts from the more flexible principles of "equity," discussed below.

The common law, significantly, denotes the principles of law as they have been evolved over time through the judicial process. Thus, William Blackstone referred to this component of English law as "*lex non scripta*"[18] – unwritten law – as opposed to the written law of legislation – statutes – enacted by Parliament or in Canada by any of the provincial

17 David M Walker, *The Oxford Companion to Law* (Oxford: Clarendon Press, 1980) at 253.

18 William Blackstone, *Commentaries on the Laws of England*, Volume 1 (Chicago: University of Chicago Press) at 63.

legislatures as well. We will have more to say about the role and construction of statutes in chapter 7.

The common law is today sometimes referred to as "case law," a term that even the judges of our highest courts have often used. The expression "case law" highlights the fact that the common law can be divined only from judgments and orders of the courts articulated in specific litigated cases. It is for this reason that the common law is sometimes thought to refer to "judge *made*" law . . . although it might be more apt to say it is "judge articulated" or "judge expressed" law. Judges are meant to apply existing principles in a way that ensures, to the greatest extent possible, that like cases are decided alike. But the common law is not stagnant, either. Nor should it be. There is little doubt that one of the important advantages of the common law system is that, in the hands of prudent and skilled judges, the law is able to advance incrementally as society's expectations and community values change, and so judges play an undeniably critical role in moving the common law forward.

TN: And what about "equity"? Is there a technical meaning for equity that is different from the dictionary definition of "fair and impartial"?

CN: Yes, the word "equity" also has a very specific technical meaning in the common law world. Historically, the common law in England was administered by courts that evolved to adjudicate disputes that would once have been brought to the King to resolve. By the end of about the thirteenth century there were three such courts: the Court of Common Pleas, the Court of King's Bench, and the Exchequer Court. Each of these courts had jurisdiction over different types of disputes, the details of which have been explored at length by legal historians.

The critical point for our purposes is that the common law seemed to involve the application of strict, rigid rules, which, in particular circumstances, could lead to results that seemed contrary to reason or were simply unfair. As the early common law judges in England confined themselves to specifically recognized forms of action, with no purported discretion to grant remedies beyond the narrow parameters of these forms of actions, aggrieved persons came to petition the King for relief from the rigidities of the common law courts. Jurisdiction to deal with these sorts of petitions was delegated to the chancellor and, over time, further delegated to a specialized court: the Court of Chancery. As the Oxford *Companion to Law* explains, "Equity grew up to supply the defects and correct the injustices of the common law."[19]

The Court of Chancery originally had its own jurisdiction, dealing, for example, with such matters as trusts. And the types of remedies available at law (from the common law courts) and in equity (from the Court of Chancery) were also different. For example, courts of law could typically order only money damages, while equitable remedies included mandatory orders such as injunctions (preventing people from taking certain actions) and orders for specific performance (to compel people to take certain actions). But the relative roles and authority of the courts of common law

19 Walker, above note 17 at 425.

and equity were confronted directly in the early seventeenth century.

In 1616 – the same year that William Shakespeare died, incidentally – Sir Edward Coke, the chief justice of the common law Court of King's Bench, clashed with Lord Chancellor Baron Ellesmere of the Court of Chancery over the putative power of the Court of Chancery to effectively overturn a decision of the Court of King's Bench. The specific question at the centre of the Coke/Ellesmere dispute turned on the interpretation of two statutes that appeared to prohibit any attempt by anyone (including, perhaps, any court) to challenge a decision of the Court of King's Bench. The question was referred to a panel of the King's advisers who determined that neither of the two statutes in question applied to decisions of the Court of Chancery. In other words, decisions of the Court of King's Bench could, indeed, be effectively undone by the Court of Chancery. Equity was thus to prevail over law.[20]

TN: Do we still have separate common law courts and equity (or Courts of Chancery) in Canada today?

CN: There are no longer separate courts of law and equity in Canada, or in the UK either, for that matter. But the notional distinction between law and equity still continues. In the UK, the *Supreme Court of Judicature Act, 1873* consolidated the High Court of Chancery, the Court of Queen's Bench, the Court of Common Pleas, the Court of

20 For an account of the Coke/Ellesmere dispute, see John P Dawson, "Coke and Ellesmere Disinterred: The Attack on the Chancery in 1616" (1941–42) 36:2 Ill L Rev 127.

Exchequer, the High Court of Admiralty, the Court of Probate, the Court for Divorce and Matrimonial Causes, and the London Court of Bankruptcy into a single Supreme Court of Judicature. What this meant, among other things, is that from that point forward both law and equity were to be administered by the same court (in other words, by the same judges) but in accordance with specific rules laid down in section 24 of the Act. Similar legislation was also enacted by provinces in Canada.[21] Thus, Canadian superior courts, like their British counterparts, are also empowered to grant both legal and equitable remedies today, although the principles to be applied by the courts when granting legal remedies and equitable remedies remain distinct.

Private Law

TN: *The National Requirement also refers to private law, public law, and Indigenous law. The term "private law" is curious. It is obviously not referring to law that is confidential or hidden from view. Is there a simple way of understanding and distinguishing between private law and public law?*

CN: The exact meaning and scope of the terms "private law" and "public law" are the subject of considerable academic commentary and debate. But at the risk of oversimplification, one may say that the term "private law" is used to refer to the law that governs relationships between individual

21 See, e.g., Ontario *Judicature Act, 1881*, 44 Vic c 5.

citizens. "Public law," on the other hand, deals with the constitution of the state itself and the relationship between the state and private citizens. The National Requirement provides specific examples of private law, including the law of contracts, torts, and property.

TN: Contract law and tort law are both featured regularly in popular lawyer dramas like Suits. *So it's tempting to think that law school courses on those subjects will be at least a little familiar. But let's start with contracts. What might I expect to see in a law school contracts course?*

Contracts

CN: The law of contracts is essential to commercial activity. People must be able to voluntarily make agreements that they can rely on the law to enforce and that others can therefore rely upon. The law of contracts deals with the principles upon which the law will interpret and enforce obligations to which parties have voluntarily committed themselves. To distinguish between the sorts of voluntary promises or statements that create legally enforceable obligations and those that don't, the courts have developed a number of more or less flexible rules, tests, and necessary contractual elements. Students in introductory courses on contract law are bound to learn about the basic elements of a legally binding contract: that there must be an offer (and what an "offer" might entail), that the offer must be accepted (and what might constitute "acceptance"), and that there must generally be "consideration" – in other words something in some form must be received by the promisor or given or sacrificed by or on behalf of the promisee in order for the promise to be legally binding . . .

TN: *This was literally in an episode of* Suits. *Ok, sorry. Please continue.*

CN: The reason that "consideration" has featured so significantly in Anglo-Canadian contract law in the past is that purely gratuitous promises may well bind a person's conscience but are not usually the sort of promises that are intended to be enforceable as a matter of law. Contract law is principally concerned with the enforceability of agreements of a commercial nature. At least that's a rough starting point. But there are many important questions. What, exactly, will constitute an offer to someone? Can a legally significant offer be made to "all the world" through, say, a newspaper ad? There is an amusing old case on this issue that often features in first-year law school contracts courses: *Carlill v Carbolic Smoke Ball Company.*[22] The defendant company had placed an advertisement for an influenza remedy in a newspaper. The advertisement offered to pay £100 to anyone who contracted influenza after using one of the company's "smoke balls" in accordance with its instructions. I'm sure you can guess who the plaintiff was – a person who used the smoke ball, contracted influenza, and was dismayed to discover that the company was not prepared to honour its promise to pay £100 after all, asserting that this was not a genuine offer, but "mere puff."

22 [1893] 1 QB 256.

TN: What did the court decide? Was it a contract, or was the Smoke Ball Company just puffing?

CN: It was held to be a contract, both by the Court of Queen's Bench and by the Court of Appeal. So, under the right circumstances, one can make an offer to all the world that may be accepted by anyone. But how does someone indicate acceptance of an offer? That is another fundamental aspect of contract law. For example, can texting a "thumbs up" emoji constitute acceptance?[23] Can an offeror revoke an offer before it is accepted? What counts as "consideration"? Does it have to be something of real value? Is something as trivial as, say, a peppercorn enough? In what other sorts of unusual circumstances will the courts be prepared to conclude there was "consideration"? What if a promise is made without consideration (in the conventional sense of some form of payment) but another party has taken costly actions or incurred expenses to their detriment in reliance on that promise? And how, exactly, should damages be calculated when there has been a breach of contract? These are only a few of the many interesting and challenging questions that students in an introductory course on contract law will need to contend with. Of course, there are many more challenging issues in contractual interpretation that continue to be debated by lawyers, scholars, and judges.[24]

---

23 *Achter Land & Cattle Ltd v South West Terminal Ltd*, 2024 SKCA 115. At the date of writing, an application to appeal this decision to the Supreme Court of Canada is pending.

24 One especially interesting issue relates to the extent to which courts may or should consider the circumstances surrounding the creation of a contract when it

Because contracts do relate to agreements, promises, and commitments of some sort, students often grapple with the relationship between what role, if any, moral considerations should have in determining a person's legal obligation to honour a supposed contract.[25] Many years ago a very famous American judge, Oliver Wendell Holmes, Jr, commented on this aspect of American contract law. He said that "Nowhere is the confusion between legal and moral ideas more manifest than in the law of contract."[26] As a matter of law, he said, entering into a contract does not mean one is honour bound to perform it, come what may. That might well be what a moral duty would look like. But that is not what a contractual obligation means. Instead, Holmes said, "The duty to keep a contract at common law means a prediction that you must pay damages if you do not keep it – and nothing else."[27] Put another way, a promisor can always choose to pay damages instead of perform the contractual obligation, and as long as the damages are sufficient, the law neither asks nor expects anything more.

This idea – that choosing to dishonour a contract and pay damages instead is not only seen as acceptable as a matter of law but should actually be encouraged when it is efficient

seeks to determine the intent of the parties to the contract. See, e.g., *Sattva Capital Corp v Creston Moly Corp*, 2014 SCC 53.

25 Philosophy students will also be aware of Immanuel Kant's theory of contracts, but Kant's ideas go well beyond the scope of this short book. See, e.g., B Sharon Byrd, "Kant's Theory of Contract" (1997) 36 Southern J Phil 131.

26 Oliver Wendell Holmes, Jr, "The Path of the Law" (1897) 10 Harv L Rev 457 at 462.

27 *Ibid* at 462.

to do so – is often referred to today, especially by law and economics scholars, as the notion of "efficient breach." And efficient breach has been described by Columbia Law Professor Avery Katz as "the most influential concept in the economic analysis of contract law."[28]

It is not just law professors who have argued that people should not be discouraged from dishonouring contractual promises when, to paraphrase Shakespeare, such a promise "is more efficient in the breach than in the observance." The Supreme Court of Canada has explicitly endorsed the idea that the courts should not discourage efficient breach of contract.[29] So all contracts would seem to become merely agreements to either "honour or pay" at the option of the promisor.

Yet, the divide between the law of contracts and basic morality is not quite so stark as Justice Holmes implies. The Supreme Court of Canada has also held that "there is a common law duty which applies to all contracts to act honestly in the performance of contractual obligations."[30] So, there are still many important features to be mapped at the boundary between ethical and legal duties. Those

28 Avery Katz, "Virtue Ethics and Efficient Breach" (2012) 45 Suffolk L Rev 777 at 777. Professor Katz goes on to point out that the concept of efficient breach has been criticized by those who say "it violates deontological ethics" – a charge he attempts to refute.

29 *Bank of America v Mutual Trust*, 2002 SCC 43 at para 31: "Efficient breach is what economists describe as a Pareto optimal outcome where one party may be better off but no one is worse off, or expressed differently, nobody loses. *Efficient breach should not be discouraged by the courts.*" [Emphasis added.]

30 *Bhasin v Hrynew*, [2014] 3 SCR 494 at para 33.

intriguing issues we must leave here for readers to further contemplate, investigate, and debate on their own.

Torts

TN: *Your discussion of law and morality in contracts brings to mind the philosophical debate between deontology and consequentialism. I don't recall either of those terms coming up in either* Suits *or* Legally Blonde, though. *But let's turn to the second important societal obligation. You've described contract law basically as the law dealing with voluntary obligations. The other important sort of "obligations," I suppose, are involuntary, or at least those that don't arise from any failure to honour an agreement. That, I assume, is what the law of torts is about?*

CN: The law of torts concerns actions for civil wrongs. The word "tort" comes from a medieval Latin word meaning "wrong" or "injustice." Some torts are intentional in nature and so involve the same sort of wrongful behaviour that could also be prosecuted under criminal law, such as assault and battery (although there are technical differences between criminal law and tort law with respect to these matters).

Unlike criminal law, however, tort law is concerned with the rights (and corresponding obligations) of individuals to one another, rather than a person's broader duty to society or the prevention of social harms or punishment for inflicting them. So, for example, when one person sues another person alleging that their negligence caused some physical harm, the person suing is seeking monetary damages to compensate them for their particular injuries. They are not seeking to have the defendant fined or sent to jail. Those sorts of punishments are within the realm of criminal law, not tort law.

The study of tort law involves nuanced consideration of the circumstances under which an injured person may seek compensation for harms inflicted upon them and from whom, the theories upon which such compensation may be justified, and a multitude of other complicating factors relating both to liability and to available remedies.

Property

TN: Hmmm . . . like breaking your ankle at work and suing would be considered tort law. Very interesting. What about the law of property? How does it differ from contract law? It seems that they both have to do with the legal recognition of voluntary, commercial relationships of some kind.

CN: The law of property deals with how the law defines and delimits "ownership" – of such tangible things as goods and land and such intangible things as intellectual property. A study of property law challenges some of our most fundamental ideas about what it means to "own" something. For example, suppose a car owner purports to sell their car to a buyer that the owner believes they recognize as a well-known television star. The title to the car, however, is not supposed to pass to the buyer until payment is made in full, but the buyer is permitted to take possession of the car immediately. Inside the car are the ownership documents. Sadly, the "buyer" was not the real television star, after all. In fact, he turned out to be a rogue. The rogue then sells the car to an unsuspecting third party who pays full value for the car, relying in good faith on the valid ownership documents that the rogue had in their possession, documents the rogue was able to deliver to the purchaser to "prove" that they were, indeed, the owner of the car.

Of course, what the rogue has done is illegal and disgraceful and they should be made to answer for it. But suppose the rogue has managed to escape to parts unknown and cannot be found. As between the original owner and the good-faith third-party buyer, who should now be entitled to have the car? Perhaps it seems obvious that it should be returned to the original owner. After all, the original owner was simply the innocent victim of the rogue. But wasn't the buyer of the car equally an innocent victim? In fact, in some ways, one might even suggest that the buyer was perhaps even *more* innocent. The buyer did everything possible to protect themself. The original owner, in some ways, made the theft possible by willingly (if mistakenly) giving the rogue possession of the car and all the ownership documents. How could commercial transactions be carried out efficiently if good-faith buyers cannot rely on genuine documents that are delivered to them? How should the law fairly adjudicate the interests of these two competing, equally innocent parties?[31]

31 This hypothetical example is very loosely based on a combination of two English cases: *Newtons of Wembley Ltd v Williams*, [1964] 3 All ER 532 and *Lewis v Averay*, [1972] 1 QB 198. Cases such as this test the limits of a traditional property rule: *nemo dat quod non habet* (no one can give (or sell) what they do not have (or own). This bedrock principle of property law must sometimes yield to competing concerns for commercial certainty. This sort of issue is also referred to in provincial

There are other fundamental notions of property and property law that are often dealt with in law school. For example, how are property rights in something first created? Who gets to be the very first owner of something, and why does our legal system recognize such ownership rights?[32]

Property law – together with contract law – is a cornerstone of our current economic system. The principles of property law, developed before the advances of modern technology, must now be applied to ever more novel types of intangible assets and intellectual property, making property law a field characterized by ingenuity and innovation.

Public Law

TN: *You've talked about the three principal fields of private law – contracts, torts, and property. These all seem to have to do with rights and obligations of various kinds between individual citizens, but where those rights and obligations are subject to adjudication by the courts and enforcement by the state if necessary. So they don't seem to be entirely "private," do they? But what about the other side of the private/public law coin? What is covered by the concept of "public law"?*

CN: Public law, as distinguished from private law, refers to the laws governing the relationship between individuals and the

sale of goods legislation. See, e.g., Ontario's *Sale of Goods Act*, RSO 1990, c S.1, s 22; see also the *Factors Act*, RSO 1990, c F.1, s 2.

32 A very old law school case that raises some of these issues is *Pierson v Post* (1805) 3 Caines 175, an American case that involves the alleged property interest a fox hunter has in the hunted fox.

state, as opposed to the relationship of individuals to one another. The National Requirement refers in particular to the following three important public law topics:

- Constitutional law
- Criminal law
- Administrative law

Each of these topics is wide-reaching and complex, so even a rudimentary introduction to these subjects would call for a far greater level of detail and expertise than can be offered in this short chapter (or by these authors).

We will offer only these few cursory words of explanation.

Constitutional Law

Canadian constitutional law deals with the fundamental and constitutive elements of the Canadian government structure and the fundamental rights and freedoms of the people in Canada. The Canadian Constitution comprises both written documents and unwritten conventions. Among the most foundational written documents are the *Constitution Act, 1867* and the *Constitution Act, 1982,* which includes the *Canadian Charter of Rights and Freedoms.*

The *Constitution Act, 1867* was a statute originally called the *British North America Act.* It was enacted by the British Parliament for the purpose of providing for the union of the original provinces of Canada into a single "Dominion." The *British North America Act* took effect on July 1, 1867, and it is that event, of course, that is celebrated each year on "Canada Day."

One of the critical elements of the federal state created by this union was the distribution of legislative powers between the Parliament of Canada, on the one hand, and the individual provincial legislatures on the other. Parliament was to have exclusive legislative authority over certain matters (for example, banks, railways, currency and coinage, postal service), and the provincial legislatures were to have exclusive authority over other matters (for example, local works and undertakings, property and civil rights in the province, the administration of justice in the province) Disputes over the interpretation of this distribution of legislative authority have arisen throughout the course of Canada's history, and the principles upon which courts have adjudicated these disputes constitute a significant part of Canadian constitutional law and the notion of Canadian federalism.

A watershed event in Canadian constitutional law occurred in 1982 when the Canadian Constitution was "patriated." By that time, Canada's de facto autonomy as a sovereign state had been indisputably established for many decades. Yet Canada's written Constitution was an anomaly: The *British North America Act* was a statute of a foreign country – the United Kingdom – that could, as a technical matter, be amended only by the UK Parliament. The patriation of the Canadian Constitution in 1982 was the culmination of a series of challenging political events, including a 1980 referendum in the province of Quebec on a proposal for "sovereignty association" with (which essentially meant "separation from") the rest of Canada. Though the referendum was defeated, it seemed clear that the terms of the existing Canadian federation had become unsatisfactory to a significant segment of the population. The federal government, under the leadership of then Prime Minister Pierre Trudeau, initiated the steps that would lead to the establishment of our current constitutional regime.

A resolution was introduced in the Canadian Parliament consisting of a joint "address" to Queen Elizabeth by the House of Commons and the Senate of Canada. That address requested the Queen "to lay before the UK Parliament" a statute – the *Canada Act 1982*. The *Canada Act 1982* was a very short piece of legislation. It consisted of a brief (73-word) preamble and just four short sections. The first section enacted a second accompanying document, the *Constitution Act, 1982,* as the law of Canada. The *Constitution Act, 1982,* which established Canada's new constitutional regime, including the new *Canadian Charter of Rights and Freedoms,* was included as a Schedule to the *Canada Act 1982*. The second section of the *Canada Act* then declared that "No Act of the Parliament of the United Kingdom passed after the *Constitution Act, 1982* comes into force shall extend to Canada as part of its law." So the *Canada Act 1982* was to be the last piece of UK legislation that would ever apply to Canada. From that point forward, any changes to Canada's written Constitution would be made in Canada by Canadians in accordance with the amending formulae set out in the new *Constitution Act, 1982*. The Canadian Constitution had thus been patriated – brought home to Canada.

At the time, some legal commentators wondered if, as a technical matter, it was actually possible for the UK Parliament to give up its authority to legislate for Canada permanently. The basis for this argument was that there is a general principle that no parliament can bind a future parliament. Since, from the UK perspective, the *Canada Act 1982* was an ordinary statute passed by the UK Parliament, on this theory a future parliament could simply repeal that Act. However, a number of leading constitutional law experts reasoned that the *Canada Act 1982* did effectively (and permanently) remove the authority of the UK Parliament to enact legislation effective in Canada.

TN: So the Canadian Charter of Rights and Freedoms first came into force in 1982 and is really part of another act, the Constitution Act, 1982, which is, somehow, not just an ordinary piece of legislation but is a constitutionally entrenched document.

CN: Yes, the *Constitution Act, 1982,* as formally enacted by the *Canada Act 1982,* thus provided the structure for Canada's new patriated Constitution. The *Constitution Act, 1982* also included for the first time a written declaration of fundamental rights and freedoms: the *Canadian Charter of Rights and Freedoms* (the "Charter").

TN: I mean, it does seem that it kind of took us long enough, don't you think? Did the Canadian Charter of Rights create new rights for Canadians, or did it just formally, constitutionally recognize rights and freedoms that Canadians already had?

CN: Certainly, Canada had always been a free and democratic country "with a Constitution similar in Principle to that of the United Kingdom,"[33] as the *British North America Act* had always affirmed, and indisputably is one of the world's most prominent liberal democracies. But the Charter still represented a major development. The Charter comprises the first 34 sections of the *Constitution Act, 1982.* Including an express charter of rights of freedoms within a constitutional

33 *Constitution Act, 1867*, 30 & 31 Vict, c 3, reprinted in RSC 1985, Appendix II, No 5, preamble.

document was new for Canada and was highly significant. Canada had for many years before 1982 had a Bill of Rights,[34] and Canadian provinces had enacted human rights codes for the protection of human rights in their respective provinces. But these earlier rights protections were all contained in "ordinary" statutes. They could be amended or repealed at any time, perhaps, for example, in response to ephemeral populist whims.

The Charter was different. As a constitutionally entrenched document, it could only be amended through special amending procedures included in the *Constitution Act, 1982*. Those procedures were – by design – very difficult to satisfy and required much greater measure of agreement between the federal government and provincial governments than is necessary to amend ordinary statutes.

The new regime also significantly enhanced the role of Canadian courts. Section 52 of the *Constitution Act, 1982* declared that

> The Constitution of Canada is the supreme law of Canada, and any law that is inconsistent with the provisions of the Constitution is, to the extent of the inconsistency, of no force or effect.

Canadian courts, therefore, now had not only the authority but also the constitutionally enshrined responsibility to ensure that Canadian laws adhered to the Constitution – including the Charter. To the extent that laws were not

34 *Canadian Bill of Rights*, S.C. 1960, c. 44.

consistent with the Charter, the courts could (and would) strike down those laws and declare them to be of no force or effect.

Of course, the rights and freedoms guaranteed by the Charter are not intended to be absolute. Section 1 of the Charter expressly declares that the Charter's rights and freedoms are "subject only to such reasonable limits prescribed by law as can be demonstrably justified in a free and democratic society." Nevertheless, the interpretation of the scope of the rights themselves as well as the limits imposed by section 1 falls to the courts.

TN: It seems like judges in Canada just gained a lot of power, then?

CN: That very impact was well understood at the time the 1982 constitutional changes were being debated. In fact, the prospect that unelected judges would now have the authority to strike down legislation enacted by democratically elected legislatures greatly disturbed some early critics of the new constitutional regime. This power seemed, in their view, to run counter to longstanding Canadian traditions of Parliamentary sovereignty or supremacy. So the *Constitution Act, 1982* provided a partial compromise (a compromise that has itself been the subject of continuing debate and disagreement). The partial compromise was this: The Charter includes a sort of "override power" that permits Parliament or the provincial legislatures, as the case may be, to enact legislation that expressly declares that the legislation will operate notwithstanding some of the Charter's provisions. Contrary to what you might occasionally read in the news media about this "notwithstanding clause," not all of the Charter provisions can be overridden in this way. Voting rights and mobility rights and some language rights in the Charter, for example, cannot be overridden by Parliament or the provincial legislatures. But some of the most important Charter rights are subject to the notwithstanding clause, including the "equality rights" set out in section 15 of the Charter.

The "notwithstanding" clause has never been used by Parliament,[35] although it has been invoked in some provincial legislation. We also see, from time to time, provincial governments and some federal politicians publicly announcing that they may be prepared to use the "notwithstanding" clause to enact legislation in circumstances where they consider it essential to enact proposed legislation that may impact certain fundamental rights and freedoms.

Canadian constitutional law, including the nuances of the Charter, is one of the most intriguing, intellectually rewarding, and practically important subjects that a student has the chance to explore at law school.

TN: I mean, don't understate things here. Tell us how you really feel about the Charter.

Criminal Law

TN: Another important part of public law is criminal law. Criminal law seems to be the area of law most familiar to non-lawyers. Criminal law and criminal law trials are featured in many books, movies, and television programs – both fictional works and "true crime" documentaries. I'm 99 percent sure that

35 See Government of Canada, "Section 33 – Notwithstanding Clause," online: https://www.justice.gc.ca/eng/csj-sjc/rfc-dlc/ccrf-ccdl/check/art33.html.

defending people accused of committing crimes is what most people think of when they picture what lawyers do. All of these portrayals really focus on the drama of trials and the risk of wrongly convicting innocent people or, alternatively, wrongly acquitting guilty people. But I'm not sure they deal very much in any detailed way with criminal law itself.

CN: Let's start with some basic facts about criminal law. In Canada, criminal law is one of those matters within the exclusive legislative authority of Parliament. It is one of the "classes of subject" listed in section 91 of the *Constitution Act, 1867*. So only Parliament – the federal level of government – can pass legislation dealing with criminal law. The main federal criminal law statute is the *Criminal Code*,[36] although the federal government's criminal law power is also the basis for a few aspects of some other federal statutes that include offence provisions, such as the *Competition Act*.[37] The *Criminal Code* is a long and detailed statute. It includes not only detailed descriptions of minor and major criminal offences, but also procedural rules for the prosecution of criminal offences.

As lengthy and complex as the *Criminal Code* may be, some of the most fundamental aspects of Canadian criminal law are not found in the Code itself but are part of the common law. For example, to be convicted of the most serious criminal offences in Canada, it is not enough for the prosecutors to prove that an accused has committed the physical "act" that constitutes the crime (the *actus reus*,

36 RSC 1985, c C-46.
37 RSC 1985, c C-34.

a Latin phrase meaning "guilty act"). The prosecutor must also prove that the accused had the intent to commit that act – a guilty mind (typically referred to using the Latin phrase *mens rea*). The requirement that conviction for a serious criminal offence requires proof of both the *actus reus* and the *mens rea* derives from a longer Latin maxim: *Actus non facit reum, nisi mens sit rea* ("the act does not make one guilty unless the mind is guilty"). This maxim was cited by Sir Edward Coke in 1603 in *Beverley's Case*.[38] The phrase apparently originates not, as one might have expected (given that it is expressed in Latin), from Roman law, but rather from a sermon of St Augustine on the *Epistle of James* (James 5:12).[39]

TN: *The concepts of* actus reus *and* mens rea *are actually quite familiar. (If readers also think they sound familiar, that may be because there is a discussion of* actus reus *and* mens rea *in a scene from* Legally Blonde. *Yes, my mind also went there (again). You are not alone.)*

CN: The rationale for requiring proof of *mens rea* at first seems straightforward and sensible. As a society, we want to punish deliberate wrongdoing, not accidental mistakes. There is a world of difference between accidentally running into a pedestrian with your car on a dark rainy evening and deliberately chasing down and running over someone in a fit of road rage, even though the extent of the injuries suffered by the victims could be identical in both cases.

38 (1603), 4 Co Rep 123, 117 ER 1118.

39 Sir Frederick Pollock & Frederic William Maitland, *The History of English Law Before Edward I*, Vol II (Cambridge: Cambridge University Press) at 476, note 5.

TN: In the first example, an injured person might still be able to sue for damages, though, wouldn't they? In other words, even if no crime has been committed, there might still be a tort.

CN: Yes, if the driver was negligent, that might well be the case. *Mens rea* has no role in determining tort liability of that sort. But let's return to criminal law. Once we accept that a person should be convicted of a crime only if the prosecutor is able to prove not only the commission of a culpable act but also that the accused had the requisite *mens rea*, a host of difficult and controversial challenges arise. What if a person who is accused of harming someone else was so intoxicated at the time that it was not possible for them to have formed the mental intent to commit the harmful act? Should they escape conviction or punishment? What if someone committed a terribly harmful act while their ability to make deliberative decisions was diminished in some other way? For example, suppose they were sleepwalking?[40] In the case of an offence such as sexual assault, in which an act is illegal if, and only if, one person does not consent to the act, what if the accused honestly (but mistakenly) believed the other person had consented? What risks to personal safety, individual security and dignity, and societal peace arise if we begin to interpret the requirement of the prosecutor to prove *mens rea* too strictly?

40 This is not merely a hypothetical example. There is actually a Canadian case in which a person killed one person and seriously injured another but was acquitted essentially on the basis that these acts were committed while the accused was sleepwalking. See *R v Parks*, [1992] 2 SCR 871.

We certainly never wish any innocent person to be convicted of an offence they did not commit. But we also need a criminal law system that maintains social order and ensures that people are protected, and feel protected, from the malicious and harmful actions of others. These are some of the difficult issues that judges, legal scholars, and law students must grapple with in the criminal law field.

Administrative Law

TN: The reference to "administrative law" in the National Requirement seems to be the least familiar, at least to me. What is meant by administrative law, and why is it important for law students to learn about it?

CN: Administrative law refers broadly to the legal principles governing the exercise of statutory powers of decision making by government agencies and tribunals. As the size and scope of government have grown throughout the twentieth and twenty-first centuries, the role of specialized administrative agencies and tribunals has also grown. Administrative law has thus become very important as well. There are a number of important fundamental matters dealt with in administrative law, such as ensuring that decisions are made in accordance with principles of natural or fundamental justice. A key issue in administrative law is the basis on which courts may review and, if necessary, overturn the decisions of tribunals or administrative agencies. As it happens, there have been some recent and quite important decisions by the Supreme Court of

Canada on this subject.[41] (One of these cases was described by a former justice of the Supreme Court of Canada as a "transformative"[42] decision.) Administrative law is a field of highly significant and growing importance and so, understandably, is recognized in the National Requirement as a key part of a sound legal education.

The Process of Statutory Construction and Analysis

TN: *Many of the areas of law we've discussed seem to involve reading decisions made by judges. But the National Requirement also says that law students need to learn how to interpret statutes.*

CN: At one time, the study of law in Canada was primarily the study of the common law, the legal principles developed and articulated by judges as they adjudicated individual disputes through the application and sometimes incremental modification of legal rules worked out in earlier, similar cases. Statutes – that is, legislation enacted by Parliament or by provincial legislatures – were far less voluminous and far less important than they are today. Now, however, statutes and various forms of subordinate legislation, such as regulations, have become important in almost every aspect

41 See, e.g., *Canada (Minister of Immigration and Citizenship) v Vavilov*, 2019 SCC 65; *Bell Canada v Canada (Attorney General)*, 2019 SCC 66; *TransAlta Generation Partnership v Alberta*, 2024 SCC 37; *Auer v Auer*, 2024 SCC 36.

42 *Newfoundland and Labrador Nurses' Union v Newfoundland and Labrador (Treasury Board)*, 2011 SCC 62, per Justice Abella. The case Justice Abella described as a "transformative decision" in administrative law was *Dunsmuir v New Brunswick*, 2008 SCC 9.

of Canadian life. And so it is more essential than ever that lawyers become adept at interpreting and analyzing statutes. This task is not always an easy one.

Courts have developed various "rules" or "maxims" or "canons of construction" over the years concerning how to interpret statutory language. Some of these so-called rules were traditionally expressed in Latin, which perhaps gave them a greater patina of respectability than they might really deserve. We will have a little more to say about these old rules and the modern Canadian approach to statutory interpretation later in chapter 7.

Indigenous Law

TN: *It seems that Aboriginal and Indigenous law have also become critical components of the Canadian law school curriculum. The National Requirement refers to their importance many times.*

CN: Yes, it is obvious from a reading of the FLSC's National Requirement how important an understanding of Indigenous law and legal orders and Aboriginal law have become to the curricula of Canadian law schools. Although many Canadian law schools had taken steps in the past to address these issues, a broader systematic approach has been endorsed since the publication of the Truth and Reconciliation Commission's Calls to Action in 2015.[43]

---

43 See Truth and Reconciliation Commission of Canada, "Calls to Action" (2015), online (pdf): https://ehprnh2mwo3.exactdn.com/wp-content/uploads/2021/01/Calls_to_Action_English2.pdf.

The Truth and Reconciliation Commission (TRC) was created pursuant to the *Indian Residential Schools Settlement Agreement*[44] reached in May 2006 between the Government of Canada, various religious organizations that operated Indian Residential Schools (a term defined in the agreement) in Canada, class action claimants, and the Assembly of First Nations and Inuit representatives. The TRC conceived reconciliation in terms of "establishing and maintaining a mutually respectful relationship between Aboriginal and non-Aboriginal peoples in this country."[45]

The Final Report of the TRC included 94 specific Calls to Action. A number of those Calls to Action related to law, the legal profession, and Canadian law schools. In particular, Calls to Actions 27 and 28 read as follows:

> 27. We call upon the Federation of Law Societies of Canada to ensure that lawyers receive appropriate cultural competency training, which includes the history and legacy of residential schools, the *United Nations Declaration on the Rights of Indigenous Peoples*, Treaties and Aboriginal rights, Indigenous law, and Aboriginal–Crown relations. This will require skills-based training in intercultural competency, conflict resolution, human rights, and anti-racism.
>
> 28. We call upon law schools in Canada to require all law students to take a course in Aboriginal people and the law, which includes the history and legacy of residential schools, the

44 Online (pdf): https://www.residentialschoolsettlement.ca/IRS%20Settlement%20 Agreement-%20ENGLISH.pdf.

45 Truth and Reconciliation Commission of Canada, *Honouring the Truth, Reconciling for the Future*, online (pdf): https://ehprnh2mw03.exactdn.com/wp-content /uploads/2021/01/Executive_Summary_English_Web.pdf at 6.

> *United Nations Declaration on the Rights of Indigenous Peoples,* Treaties and Aboriginal rights, Indigenous law, and Aboriginal–Crown relations. This will require skills-based training in intercultural competency, conflict resolution, human rights, and anti-racism.

These Calls to Action have been taken up by the FLSC and Canadian law schools and, as we see from the list of first-year law school courses in Appendix B, all Canadian common law schools now include material intended to integrate materials, perspectives, and cultural competency training identified in the TRC Calls to Action. One law school, the University of Victoria Faculty of Law, has even introduced a four-year transsystemic JD/JID joint degree program in common law and Indigenous legal orders.

TN: We've focused in this chapter almost entirely on the content of the first-year curriculum at Canadian common law schools. But the JD program is a three-year program. What, at least generally speaking, can students expect in the second and third year of a law school program?

CN: There is a much greater variety and diversity of courses in the upper years of law school. Although some law schools structure their degree programs such that a few mandatory courses are taken by students in their second or third years, rather than in the first year, for the most part law students have significant freedom in their upper years to design a program tailored to their own individual preferences.

They may choose to take more specialized courses, perhaps including advanced versions of one or more of the mandatory courses they took in first year. There will also be a much greater opportunity in the upper years for students who wish to do so to take courses taught by experienced practitioners teaching on a part-time or "adjunct" basis, rather than by full-time law professors.

And there are also many other types of enriching experiences that can be undertaken for course credit, including mooting or other "experiential" activities (as we discuss further in chapter 9), working with clients at the "clinics" that are now a standard part of most Canadian law schools, clerking on a part-time basis for a judge, or even spending an academic term as an exchange student at a university in another province or another country. The opportunities for all of these sorts of non-traditional enrichment opportunities are plentiful.

Now, there is an old saying about the three-year law school program that it is only fair to mention here. It goes like this:

> In the first year, they scare you to death.
> In the second year, they work you to death.
> In the third year, they bore you to death.

This very cynical summary of the law school experience reflects, in a humorously exaggerated way, some common anxieties and frustrations faced by law students. The first year for many law students is characterized by feelings of confusion and anxiety as they encounter what for many is a highly unfamiliar educational environment. For a number of students, the second year is marked by a relentless drive to achieve the highest grades possible, in the hopes of securing a desirable position following graduation. Then, because of the timing of the law school recruitment cycle, many law students begin their third year having obtained the assurance of an articling position to begin at the end of the academic year. With no further striving necessary to grasp their career brass ring, the motivation for these students to pursue their academic studies diligently noticeably declines.

Following an American practice, Canadian law students some years ago began to designate each of the three years of law schools by the year number followed by the letter "L." Thus, first-year students are "1Ls," second-year students are "2Ls," and third-year students are "3Ls." The suggestion that, for 3L students who have already lined up a post-graduation position, the final year is more one of recreation than dedication – a sort of third-year victory lap – has led to some law students flippantly calling it "3LOL."

Conclusion

In this chapter we have given you a very preliminary overview of the content of some of the foundational first-year courses offered at the typical Canadian law school, and a very brief glimpse at what might await students in the upper years as well. In the following chapters we will look more closely at how law at Canadian law schools is often taught and how law students might expect to have their academic performance evaluated.

Appendix B: First-Year Curriculum at Canadian Common Law Schools

Note: This chart is intended for general illustrative purposes only. Prospective law school applicants should consult the law schools in which they are interested directly for definitive, up-to-date curriculum information.

Law School	First-Year Mandatory Courses
University of Alberta Faculty of Law	• Foundations to Law • Legal Research and Writing • Contracts • Criminal Law • Torts • Constitutional Law • Property Law Source: https://www.ualberta.ca/law/programs/jd/curriculum.html
Allard School of Law – UBC	• Indigenous Settler Legal Relations • Contracts • Criminal Law & Procedure • Property Law • Torts • Introduction to Public Law and the Charter • Legal Research & Writing • Aboriginal and Treaty Rights • Advocacy Source: https://allard.ubc.ca/student-portal/jd-program/jd-first-year-curriculum
Bora Laskin Faculty of Law – Lakehead University	• Constitutional Law • Legal Research and Writing • Contract Law • Foundations of Canadian Law • Criminal Law • Property Law • Tort Law • Indigenous Law • Indigenous Perspectives Source: https://www.lakeheadu.ca/programs/departments/law/curriculum

Appendix B: First-Year Curriculum at Canadian Common Law Schools *(continued)*

University of Calgary Faculty of Law	• Foundations in Law & Justice I & II • Constitutional Law • Contracts • Legislation • Property • Torts • Crime Source: https://law.ucalgary.ca/future-students/our-jd-programs/jd
Schulich School of Law, Dalhousie University	• Introduction to Legal Ethics • Fundamentals of Public Law • Legal Research and Writing • African Nova Scotian Legal History, Issues and Critical Race Theory • Aboriginal and Indigenous Law in Context • Contracts and Judicial Decision Making • Criminal Justice: The Individual and the State • Law in its National and International Context • Property in Its Historical Context • Tort Law and Damage Compensation Source: https://www.dal.ca/faculty/law/current-students/jd-students/courses.html?gad_source=1&gclid=EAIaIQobChMI7c3_n6OhhQMV-1ZHARoiqQQsEAAYASAAEgLgKvD_BwE
University of Manitoba Faculty of Law	• Contracts • Criminal Law and Procedure • Constitutional Law • Torts and Compensation Systems • Property • Legal System • Legal Methods Source: https://catalog.umanitoba.ca/undergraduate-studies/law/juris-doctor-jd/index.html

Appendix B: First-Year Curriculum at Canadian Common Law Schools

McGill University Faculty of Law	• Contractual Obligations • Ex-Contractual Obligations/Torts • Criminal Justice • Indigenous Legal Traditions • Integration Workshop • Constitutional Law • Foundations Source: https://www.mcgill.ca/law-studies/bcljd-studies/structure/courses
University of New Brunswick Faculty of Law	• Foundations of Law • Constitutional Law • Criminal Law • Contracts • Property • Torts • Legal Research and Advocacy Source: https://www.unb.ca/fredericton/law/future/programs/juris-doctor.html
Osgoode Hall Law School – York University	• Ethical Lawyering in a Global Community • Public and Constitutional Law • Tort Law • Contract Law • Criminal Law • Introductory Lawyering Skills • Legal Process • Property Law • Perspective Option Seminar Source: https://www.osgoode.yorku.ca/programs/juris-doctor/your-flexible-jd-journey

Appendix B: First-Year Curriculum at Canadian Common Law Schools *(continued)*

University of Ottawa Faculty of Law	• Legal Foundations: Research, Strategy, Analysis • Contracts • Dispute Resolution and Professional Responsibility • Property • Law, Reconciliation and Decolonization • Criminal Law and Procedure* • Torts* • Introduction to Public Law and Constitutional Law* *First year students take one of these three mandatory courses in a small group format of approximately 18–25 students and the other two in a large group format of approximately 75–80 students. Source: https://catalogue.uottawa.ca/en/undergrad/juris-doctor-jd/#programrequirementstext
Queen's University Faculty of Law	• Introduction to Legal Skills • Indigenous and Aboriginal Law • Public Law • Constitutional Law • Contracts • Criminal Law • Property • Torts Source: https://law.queensu.ca/sites/lawwww/files/files/JD%20Forms/Degree%20Requirements%20Checklist.pdf
University of Saskatchewan College of Law	• Contracts • Criminal Law • Property I • Tort Law • Constitutional Law • Kwayeskastasowin: Setting Things Right • Legal Research and Writing • Dispute Resolution • Professionalism and Perspectives in Law Source: https://law.usask.ca/students/jd-students/current-students.php

Appendix B: First-Year Curriculum at Canadian Common Law Schools

Thompson Rivers University Faculty of Law	• Constitutional Law • Contracts • Crime: Law and Procedure • Fundamental Legal Skills Law • Administration and Policy • Property • Torts Source https://www.tru.ca/__shared/assets/Course_Book_2023-24_v57108.pdf
University of Toronto Faculty of Law	• Legal Methods • Constitutional Law • Contract Law • Criminal Law • Indigenous Peoples and the Canadian Legal System • Property Law • Tort Law • Legal Research and Writing Source: https://handbook.law.utoronto.ca/jd-academic-program/first-year-academic-program
Lincoln Alexander School of Law, Toronto Metropolitan University	• Law and Legal Methods • Legal Research and Writing • Criminal Law • Constitutional Law • Tort Law • Foundations of Legal Theory • Contract Law • Property Law • Ethics and Professionalism (Intensive) • Administrative and Regulatory Law • Indigenous and Aboriginal Law • Legal Research and Writing II Source: https://www.torontomu.ca/law/program/juris_doctor_program/#!accordion-1706848778949-year-one

Appendix B: First-Year Curriculum at Canadian Common Law Schools *(continued)*

University of Victoria Faculty of Law	• The Constitutional Law Process • The Criminal Law Process • Law, Legislation and Policy • Contracts • The Legal Process • Property • Torts • Legal Research and Writing First-year students enrolled in the University of Victoria's four-year joint degree JD/JID degree program in common law and Indigenous legal order take a somewhat different slate of first-year courses. Specifically, students in this program have five mandatory first-year courses: Transsytemic Constitutional Law; Transsytemic Criminal Law; Law, Legislation and Policy; Transsystemic Property Law; and Transsystemic Legal Processes, Research and Writing. Courses in Transsystemic Contracts and Transsytemic Torts are then mandatory second-year courses. Source: https://www.uvic.ca/calendar/undergrad/#/courses
Western University Faculty of Law	• Constitutional Law • Contracts • Criminal Law • Legal Research, Writing and Advocacy • Property • Torts • *EITHER* Legal Ethics and Professionalism *OR* Corporate Law (at the option of each student) Source: https://law.uwo.ca/future_students/jd_academic_programs/first_year_curriculum.html

Appendix B: First-Year Curriculum at Canadian Common Law Schools

University of Windsor Faculty of Law	• Property • Contracts • Access to Justice • Criminal Law and Procedure • Legal Writing and Research • Constitutional Law • Indigenous Legal Traditions • Windsor Legal Practice Simulation Source: https://www.uwindsor.ca/law/239/juris-doctor-jd

- Some schools include Indigenous law as a mandatory requirement in second year instead of first year.
- Some schools have specific mandatory requirements for upper-year students, while others don't.
- Courses at every school may change from year to year. The courses listed here are based on the website of each law school in the spring of 2025.

6

the socratic method and thinking like a lawyer

The rational study of law is still to a large extent the study of history.
– Oliver Wendell Holmes, Jr[1]

Teaching Law: The Socratic Method and Its Progeny

Law school is not the best fit for everyone. To understand whether it is likely to be a good fit for you, it may be helpful to consider not only what subjects you might expect to study at law school, as we discussed in chapter 5, but also *how* you might expect those subjects to be taught.

Years ago there was a very popular movie (and a spinoff TV show) that prospective law students throughout North America were encouraged to watch. That movie was called *The Paper Chase*. Based on a novel by John Jay Osborn, Jr, *The Paper Chase* was a fictionalized portrayal of the experience of

1 Oliver Wendell Holmes, Jr, "The Path of the Law" (1897) 10 Harv L Rev 457 at 469.

first-year students at Osborn's alma mater, the Harvard Law School. A central character in this movie was Professor Charles Kingsfield, an imperious contracts professor portrayed by the distinguished actor John Houseman. In his first appearance in the film, Professor Kingsfield stands before a classroom of cowed (or are they just bored?) first-year law students, explaining the merits of Harvard Law's favoured "Socratic method" of instruction. Students should expect no lectures in his class, he warns them. There would only be an endless series of questions for them to answer:

> *Kingsfield:* Through my questions you learn to teach yourselves. Through this method of questioning, answering, questioning, answering, we seek to develop in you the ability to analyze the vast complex of facts that constitute the relationship of members within a given society . . . You teach yourselves the law. But I train your minds.[2]

It is said that the fictional Professor Kingsfield was based on one of the actual professors encountered at Harvard by Osborn. Some Harvard Law graduates have even proudly claimed that they had been students of the "real" Professor Kingsfield, although Osborn himself denied that Kingsfield was intended to represent any one particular professor.[3] Whether based on one real professor or a composite of many, Kingsfield was, in any case, the embodiment of the "Socratic" professor,

2 James Bridges [Director], *The Paper Chase* [motion picture], 20th Century Fox, 1973.

3 Richard Sandomir, "John Jay Osborn, Jr, Author of *The Paper Chase,* Dies at 77," *New York Times* (27 October 2022).

illustrating (or perhaps caricaturing) the method of law school instruction for which Harvard Law School had become famous and which, in turn, had been emulated by law schools throughout North America.

You are not likely to meet any professor like Professor Kingsfield at a Canadian law school today (or indeed at any other law school, for that matter – including Harvard). What survives of the Socratic method is a much gentler "question-and-answer" approach to teaching, and it is by no means the sole or even primary method of instruction used by professors in most Canadian law schools. Even those professors who describe their teaching method today as "Socratic" are typically using the term to refer to a very different classroom experience from that endured by students of the traditional Socratic professors of a bygone era. In specialized upper-year law school classes, in particular, the Socratic method is probably encountered as infrequently as Socrates himself. Professors instead resort increasingly in upper-year courses to more lecture-based instruction.

But an important legacy of the Socratic/case method of law teaching survives, especially in many first-year law school courses.

TN: So what exactly is (or was) the law school version of the Socratic method? What was it intended to accomplish?

CN: The phrase "Socratic method," of course refers to the supposed teaching method used by the ancient Greek philosopher Socrates, with whom I know you are quite familiar from your philosophy studies. We don't really know much about how Socrates himself engaged with his students.

Socrates wrote nothing. Our principal source of information about Socrates comes from his rightly famous student, the philosopher Plato, whose remarkable and timeless "dialogues" portray what is surely a largely fictionalized version (or versions) of his eminent teacher. The Socrates depicted by Plato, for example in *The Republic,* uses a series of probing questions to challenge his students to reflect on and challenge their intuitions and preconceptions until they gradually arrive at answers that the students themselves recognize and acknowledge as the "truth."

TN: Which, I suppose, readers would already know if they had taken Intro to Philosophy in university. We mentioned a little about the origin of the Socratic case method at Harvard in chapter 4. But how did the Socratic method come to migrate from Harvard and acquire such a place of prominence in the pedagogy of North American law schools?

CN: To answer this question, we need to roll back the clock a little and consider the older teaching methods used in American law schools that the Socratic method came to displace.

No dynamic back-and-forth exchange of questions and answers characterized the earliest North American law schools. As we mentioned in chapter 4, at the old pre-university proprietary law schools in the United States – such as the school in Northampton, Massachusetts, or the Litchfield School in Connecticut – it appears that the form of instruction was lecturing, and those lectures were basically exercises in dictation. Instructors would read aloud to their students from their notes or perhaps textbooks. The job of the students was to copy down these oral lectures as accurately as possible. Questions from students were likely rather rare and probably limited to seeking rudimentary clarification.

TN: When was there a switch in the teaching methods?

CN: This lecture method of law teaching probably continued to be the dominant approach to teaching law in the United States in the newly evolving university-affiliated American law schools until the mid-nineteenth century. Two major innovations in law school teaching emerged around that time, as we discussed in chapter 4: one at Columbia University and the other at the Harvard Law School. Columbia's innovations were pioneered by Theodore Dwight, the first dean of Columbia's Law School. Harvard's new approach was championed by Christopher Columbus Langdell, the first dean of the Harvard Law School. Both used a Socratic style of teaching, as we have explained, a method which was, evidently, already commonly used in undergraduate programs at American colleges of the time.[4]

TN: You mentioned in chapter 4 that the two methods differed and that Dwight believed his method was superior, at least for students of "average ability." Can you elaborate a bit on the difference between the two methods?

CN: Where the two methods fundamentally differed was with respect to the materials used for study. Dwight's method focused on the principles of law as found in published

4 See Theodore W Dwight, "Columbia College Law School, New York" (1889) 1:4 Green Bag 141 at 146: "[T]he methods pursued in the Columbia Law School closely connect themselves with collegiate training. Graduates of the Colleges find substantially the same methods of education in use here to which they have been already accustomed."

texts.[5] The purpose of the "recitations" in which a student of Dwight's might participate in his class was, as Dwight himself explained, "mainly to make it certain that he has studied the subject and has in a measure comprehended it, and is thus in a position to listen with advantage to expositions."[6]

Langdell's approach and Langdell's pedagogical goal were different. Langdell believed that law was best taught through the use of inductive reasoning,[7] using as primary source material judgments of appellate courts.

TN: *It might help to clarify what you mean by the "inductive method" when you are talking about the Socratic style of law school teaching.*

CN: The inductive method essentially means observing specific examples and seeking to infer general principles that would explain, reconcile, or rationalize those specific examples. So, for Langdell's case method, that meant asking students to read the judgments or opinions usually of appellate courts and then guiding students to determine or discover the general legal principles that would account for the outcome of these decisions in a way that would render the decisions consistent with one another. Scientists use an inductive approach when they conduct experiments, record their observations, then draw general conclusions, for example, about physical laws or properties that would

5 *Ibid* at 145.
6 *Ibid* at 145.
7 However, at least one commentator has insisted that "I don't believe Langdell ever talked about an 'inductive method' in his life." See Clarence D Ashley, "The 'Failure' of Professor Langdell" (1909) 2:6 Am L Sch Rev 257 at 258.

explain these individual experimental observations. In Langdell's view, court cases were like these individual experiments or data points, and the law school library was analogous to a laboratory.[8]

Langdell's system, then, which ultimately came to influence the teaching of law throughout North America, was not characterized simply by the Socratic question-and-answer method of instruction but also by the novel use of the "case method." The case method, which came to be closely associated with Langdell himself as well as with his formalist view of law as a field of study, was not popularized until quite late in the nineteenth century.

It's important not to exaggerate the novelty of Langdell's approach. Langdell was not the first person to recognize the value of learning the law through the study of decided cases.[9] What was unique about Langdell's approach is that Langdell applied the case method not merely to the personal *study* of law (for which there was ample historical precedent) but rather that he extended the approach to the *teaching* of law.[10]

As we mentioned in chapter 4, unlike Dwight, who, by all accounts, was an extraordinarily popular and successful teacher, Langdell evidently struggled in the classroom.[11]

---

8 See, e.g., Christopher Columbus Langdell, "Teaching Law as a Science," speech before the Harvard Law Association (1887) 21:1 Am L Rev 123.

9 William Schofield, "Christopher Columbus Langdell" (1907) 55:5 Am L Reg 273 at 280.

10 *Ibid* at 280.

11 Franklin Fessenden, a student in the early years of Langdell's teaching career at Harvard, has reported that "[t]he contrast between the two methods [i.e., the old lecture method and Langdell's case method] became sharper. As time passed,

Thus, while Dwight presided over an impressively growing law school at Columbia, Langdell's early years at Harvard were contentious and initially unpromising. Yet, despite the shaky start, Langdell's Socratic "case method" of instruction was gradually recognized as a uniquely effective way of teaching law students. Perhaps this recognition occurred as strong students who had thrived under Langdell's system began to excel as practising lawyers. Perhaps the case method flourished thanks to the talent of other young Harvard Law professors who followed Langdell – notably James Barr Ames – who may have been frankly more adept classroom practitioners of Langdell's teaching method than Langdell himself.[12] Whatever the reason, the impact of Langdell's method was unmistakable, far reaching, and long lasting. Sadly, perhaps, Langdell himself was compelled to give up using the case method in his later years as a law professor as his sight failed him and he defaulted to conducting his classes by lecture instead.[13] But no matter. By then his incomparable legacy had been established.

TN: *Would we be more likely to see the Langdell Socratic case method in a Canadian classroom or Dwight's textbook method?*

CN: I can only guess at that based on conversations I have had with colleagues at other Canadian law schools. I can say that

---

fewer and fewer remained in Langdell's lectures. The number dwindled to seven or eight." See Franklin G Fessenden, "Rebirth of the Harvard Law School" (1919–20) 33:4 Harv L Rev 493 at 503.

12 Samuel Williston, for example, described Ames as "a teacher of rare skill" to whom "almost as much to Langdell . . . the success is due of the Case method of study." Samuel Williston, "James Barr Ames" (1910) 10 Colum L Rev 845 at 846.

13 William Schofield, "Christopher Columbus Langdell" (1907) 55:5 Am L Reg 273 at 277.

teaching law from textbooks would be rare in Canada and that Langdell's name, and Langdell's approach, are certainly much more well known today by Canadian law school professors than Dwight's. For example, the University of Alberta's academic calendar explains that the establishment of U of A's Faculty of Law "was inspired by changes instituted at Harvard Law School by Dean Langdell."[14] I'm not aware of any Canadian law school that pays similar homage to Dean Dwight. It is very possible that Canadian law schools were also significantly influenced by pedagogical approaches at Harvard since, for a time, a significant proportion of Canadian law professors elected to pursue their graduate law studies at the Harvard Law School before beginning their academic careers in Canada. Indeed, one leading scholar once suggested that, because of the disproportionate number of Canadian law professors who had studied at Harvard, for many years the Harvard Law School may have exerted an even greater influence on Canadian legal education than on American legal education. I would hasten to add, though, that Harvard Law's quasi-monopoly in providing graduate legal education to Canadian law professors has long since ended. One now finds significantly greater diversity in graduate degrees among members of the Canadian legal academy.

Quite apart from any disproportionate influence the Harvard Law School may or may not have had on the teaching of law at Canadian law schools, there is another reason that Dwight's method – which tended to rely on recitation

14 University of Alberta, "Faculty of Law General Information," online: https://calendar.ualberta.ca/content.php?catoid=44&navoid=13593#history-of-the-law-faculty.

of textbook principles rather than the gleaning of principles from the language of judicial decisions – would not be as warmly received by many Canadian law professors. Dwight's method seems to endorse the authoritative nature of what is sometimes dubbed "black letter law," and the teaching of black letter law has, at least in some contexts, become a target of derision on the part of many Canadian law professors.

TN: What is "black letter law"?

CN: The term "black letter law" means a legal rule or principle that is uncontentious, settled, authoritative, even trite. The phrase "black letter law" apparently refers to the text of legal rules as they once appeared in standard legal textbooks. Some people contend that, in such books, there would be some background discussion of a particular legal principle, and then the definitive "rule" itself would be printed in heavy black type. Other sources suggest that the term refers more generally to the sort of bold black Gothic type font in which all such standard legal textbooks were printed.[15] Whatever the etymology of the term, the agreed meaning of the phrase today is the same: Black letter law refers to uncontentious, dogmatic statements of legal doctrine, what some American authorities refer to as "hornbook law" – meaning a simple, uncontentious statement of settled law set out in a "hornbook," which is a subject primer for students. Beginning law students sometimes expect law school to involve learning a series of

15 See, e.g., Cornell Law School, Legal Information Institute, q.v. "blackletter law," online: https://www.law.cornell.edu/wex/blackletter_law.

straightforward "rules" that can then be applied in solving clients' problems in practice. But if law consisted of nothing more than a collection of such non-contentious, authoritative statements, it would not only be dangerously inflexible, but it would also be an arid and intellectually uninspiring topic of university study and a very mundane career option.

The Socratic Method Today

TN: So it sounds like law school is less about clear-cut "black and white" and far more about debating over shades of grey. Is some version of the Socratic method or the case method the standard way of teaching law at Canadian law schools?

CN: It remains very influential. But there is no prescribed way of teaching law at Canadian law schools. Individual professors decide for themselves what method or methods they think work best, and methods and styles of teaching are as numerous and different as the professors themselves. Some professors prefer to lecture – to perform the role, as some commentators have glibly put it, of "the sage on the stage."[16] Others prefer to surrender the classroom spotlight to others, allowing student discussion to predominate instead and intervening only when needed to facilitate or perhaps redirect or refocus discussion – playing a part sometimes facetiously described as "the guide on the side."[17]

16 See, e.g., Alison King, "From Sage on the Stage to Guide on the Side" (1993) 41:1 College Teaching 30.

17 *Ibid.*

For professors whose own legal education at some point has included exposure to some variant of the Socratic method, it is not surprising that they may choose to adopt that method in their law school classrooms as well. For some professors, this might mean asking probing questions intended to gently lead students to the "better view of the law" (namely, the view of matters held by the professor). In other cases, the questioning might be more aptly described as the "sophistic" rather than the "Socratic" method, as it is aimed not at drawing out the most convincingly reasoned view, but rather at demonstrating that there are no indisputable answers at all, and that any proposition whatsoever may be, at one moment, expressly contradicted and in the next unequivocally defended by a skilled and zealous advocate.[18]

Even among devoted "Socratic" professors, there are still many different approaches. For example, some professors insist that there is an important value to "cold calling": to call, with no advance warning, on students who have not volunteered to speak in class. (In *The Paper Chase,* the fictional Professor Kingsfield mentioned earlier employs this unforgiving technique with rather embarrassing

18 The term "sophists" refers to a group of professional educators in ancient Greece dating from around the fifth century BCE. Socrates himself was apparently wrongly accused of being a sophist. The sophists were condemned for their apparent disruptive iconoclasm and relativism. (See, e.g., Noburu Notomi, "The Sophists and Socrates: Reconsidering the History of the Criticisms of the Sophists" (2022) 11 Humanities 153.) Although the reputation of the sophists as relativists who rejcted the notion of objective truth is almost universal, Richard Bett has argued that it may actually be undeserved. See Richard Bett, "The Sophists and Relativism" (1989) 34 Phronesis 139.

consequences for an unprepared student.) Defenders of the "cold calling" technique insist that it offers significant pedagogical advantages not only for those few students who are called upon in class on any particular day but also for the many students who are not. The students in the spotlight rehearse for their future role as adviser or counsel, organizing their thoughts under pressure and honing their ability to respond with clarity, grace, eloquence, and poise. To use the tired cliché, they must, quite literally, learn to "think on their feet." For others who are spectators only, they may nevertheless take the opportunity of observing the interaction of professor and students to visualize how they might have responded – and by so doing improve their own understanding of how to read, organize, analyze, and recall legal materials effectively.

TN: *I'm not convinced that cold calling is the best method. Putting students on the spot seems to add unnecessary pressure to what is already, for many students, a stressful situation. Worse than that, worrying about being called on could actually make it more difficult for some people to concentrate and learn in the first place. I suppose if everyone in law school was planning to be a trial lawyer, cold calling might make sense. But I don't think that's the case at all.*

CN: For many of those very reasons cold calling also strikes some professors as unduly harsh or unnecessarily intimidating. They are mindful of the considerable stress the prospect of being called upon places on many students, especially students who, though perhaps of great intellectual and analytical ability, may have retiring personalities. Nor is it clear that exposing sensitive students to the rigours of cold calling can necessarily be justified as essential career preparation. The unique fear of potentially being embarrassed in front of a large group of one's peers in a law school classroom may bear little similarity to the very different types of performance challenges prospective lawyers are likely to face regularly in their careers – whether in the courtroom or the conference room.

For these reasons, some professors choose to use techniques that they hope will mitigate stress while preserving at least some of the presumed benefits of the traditional Socratic method. One technique for doing this is by using some sort of "panel" or "hot seat" system. A small group of students will be told in advance of class that members of their group will be "on call" for that day. Each member of the group is therefore expected to prepare carefully and stand ready to lead the classroom discussion when called upon. But those students whose panel is not "on call" need not worry about being called upon unless they volunteer to speak.

Yet another variant on the Socratic method is the class-by-class "opt out" approach. The idea here is that any student who wishes to do so is permitted to confidentially "opt out" of being cold called – provided that they expressly request such an "opt out" on a class-by-class basis, for example, by sending an email to this effect to the professor the night before the class. It is typically a feature of this "opt out" regime that there may be no "once and for all" passes. It is hoped that, by giving students the freedom to remove themselves from the question "firing line," they will come to feel more comfortable and in control so that, as the term progresses, their confidence will increase, fear of being called upon will subside, and they will not only willingly but enthusiastically choose to participate. The opt out option also has the advantage of giving students a better chance to manage their workload. It may not always be possible to thoroughly prepare for every one of your courses each and every day. In an opt out environment, students can rest assured that, if they aren't able to do the reading for a particular class, they can send a confidential message to the professor in advance and need not worry about being caught unprepared in class. But on those days when the topic is of especial interest to students and they have carefully read and thought about the assigned reading, it is hoped that they will not only choose not to "opt out," but that they will even feel emboldened to volunteer to answer and engage actively in class discussion.

Teaching You to "Think Like a Lawyer"

TN: Before we leave the topic of the general goal of Canadian legal education and the classroom approach of individual law professors, there is one particular idea I think we should discuss. I have seen in many different sources that the goal of law school isn't necessarily to teach you all the law. The goal is to teach you how to "think like a lawyer." If that is the goal of law school, what exactly does that mean and how does law school manage to do that?"

CN: The fictional Professor Kingsfield, whom we have referred to several times earlier in this chapter, famously proclaimed that a student would come to his class "with a skull full of mush" and would leave "thinking like a lawyer." Law students will often hear the claim that law school is intended to help them learn to "think like lawyers." This putative law school goal has been around for a very long time. There was once a famous American law professor named Karl Llewelleyn. He is remembered today among legal scholars as one of the important "legal realists" of the early part of the twentieth century. Legal realism has cast a very long shadow over North American legal education for almost 100 years.

Karl Llewellyn published a book in 1930 called *The Bramble Bush*.[19] The book was a collection of lectures. In one of those lectures, this is what Llewellyn said about the first year of law school and learning to "think like a lawyer":

> The first year, as I have already stated, aims to drill into you the more essential techniques of handling cases. It lays a foundation simultaneously for law school and law practice. It aims, in the old phrase, to get you to "think like a lawyer." The hardest job of the first year is to lop off your commonsense, to knock your ethics into temporary anesthesia. Your view of social policy, your sense of justice – to knock these out of you along with woozy thinking, along with ideas all fuzzed along their edges. You are to acquire ability to think precisely, to analyze coldly, to work within a body of materials that is given, to see, and see only, and manipulate, the machinery of the law. It is not easy thus to turn human beings into lawyers. Neither is it safe. For a mere legal machine is a social danger.[20]

19 Karl N Llewellyn, *Bramble Bush: Some Lectures on Law & Its Study* (New York: s.n., 1930).
20 *Ibid* at 102.

You can see that, even by 1930, "thinking like a lawyer" is already described by Llewellyn as "an old phrase" and as one that is already being viewed with healthy doses of caution and cynicism. So common is the assertion that law school aims to teach its students to think like lawyers that it is interesting to consider that when Christopher Columbus Langdell initiated his revolutionary teaching project at the Harvard Law School back in the nineteenth century, he evidently had a much more ambitious task in mind. Langdell seemed to be of the view that the fundamental principles of law were modest in number[21] and could actually be mastered during a law student's law school career. Langdell, in other words, seemed to believe that law school wasn't just about learning to "think like a lawyer" at all. It was about learning the law. All the law (or at least all the principles of law that mattered). That seems to us today to be a rather audacious and frankly utterly unrealistic idea, and it soon went to the resting place of all impossible ideas. In its place arose this curious and enduring notion that the law school mission is to teach students how to "think like a lawyer."

The idea that law school is about learning to "think like a lawyer" is now ubiquitous. There is a surprisingly large number of books for law students that include "Thinking Like a Lawyer" somewhere in their titles.[22] Some brave

21 Franklin G Fessenden, "Rebirth of the Harvard Law School" (1920) 33:4 Harv L Rev 493 at 506.

22 See, e.g., JA Crook, *Thinking Like a Lawyer: Essays on Legal History and General History for John Crook on His Eightieth Birthday* (Boston: Brill, 2002); Patrick M McFadden, *A Student's Guide to Legal Analysis: Thinking Like a Lawyer*

people have even purported to define this vague and mysterious concept. For example, an entry in the *Australian Law Dictionary* explains the notion this way:

> Traditionally considered positively, as the ability to reason dispassionately about legal facts and issues rather than becoming too involved in a client's case. The rationale is that a lawyer who is trained to act at arm's length and does not get drawn into the client's emotional concerns is more rational and effective in the legal arena. Thinking more critically about the meaning of 'thinking like a lawyer' is a current issue in legal education.[23]

I'm sure it won't surprise you to hear that plenty of people would dispute that particular definition, and many more have argued that law schools actually teach no such thing in any event. After all, they argue, how could they? To say that law schools can teach students to think like lawyers presumes, first, that there is a distinct type of lawyers' thinking (or legal reasoning),[24] that this distinct sort of thinking

(Gaithersburg, MD: Aspen Law and Business, 2001); Elizabeth Mertz, *The Language of Law School: Learning to Think Like a Lawyer* (Oxford: Oxford University Press, 2007); William Powers, Jr, *Sharpening the Legal Mind: How to Think Like a Lawyer* (Austin: University of Texas Press, 2023); Sarah E Redfield, *Thinking Like a Lawyer: An Educator's Guide to Legal Analysis and Research,* 2nd ed (Durham, NC: Carolina Academic Press, 2011); Frederick Schauer, *Thinking Like a Lawyer: A New Introduction to Legal Reasoning* (Cambridge, MA: Harvard University Press, 2009); Colin Searle, *Thinking Like a Lawyer: A Framework for Teaching Critical Thinking* (London: Routledge, 2021). This is a very small sample. If one were to add book chapters and articles that include "thinking like a lawyer" in the title, the list would number in the dozens.

23 Trischa Mann, ed, *Australian Law Dictionary.*

24 Schauer, *Thinking Like a Lawyer,* above note 22.

can be learned sitting in a university classroom, and, more particularly, that it can somehow be taught by people who have not themselves, for the most part, ever worked as lawyers engaged in the actual practice of law.

Of course, there might well be a distinct kind of legal reasoning. For example, we might say that "thinking like a lawyer" includes, among other things, the ability to find relevant similarities between the facts of past decided cases that are favourable to a client and a similar ability to draw fine distinctions between the facts of unfavourable past decisions and the position of one's client. A lawyer – and certainly a judge – must also be able to refrain from rushing to conclusions until all the evidence has been presented and to recognize that there is always some argument that may be made in support of a client's position, no matter how unpopular or unlikely that position (or that client) might be. But it is not entirely clear how dedicated university-affiliated law schools necessarily are to fostering that distinct sort of reasoning, especially in recent years as they have become encouraged to become increasingly "interdisciplinary."[25]

The materials usually relied upon by law professors for the task of guiding students to "think like lawyers" could also be seen as a little surprising: the text of court judgments, especially the judgments of appellate courts such as provincial courts of appeal or the Supreme Court of Canada. It is no wonder that some critics in the past have

25 For a provocative and insightful article on important aspects of this topic, see Ernest J Weinrib, "Can Law Survive Legal Education?" (2007) 60 Vand L Rev 401.

complained that law school is not trying so much to teach you to think like a lawyer – it is actually trying to teach you to think like an appellate court judge.

TN: But there must be at least some specific foundational legal principles or approaches that law students develop in law school that enable them to approach legal problems in a way that is different from the rest of us. Otherwise, requiring lawyers to go to law school for three years doesn't seem to be the best use of people's time or talents.

CN: There are certainly some basic precepts that law students learn very early on in their first year and then, if they are clever, spend the next two years regularly trying to challenge and debunk. Here are three of the most fundamental (all encapsulated in Latin phrases):

- *Stare decisis*
- *Ratio decidendi*
- *Obiter dicta*

Stare decisis literally means "to stand by what has been decided." In other words, once a court has decided a point of law, subsequent courts – notably courts ranking lower on the judicial pecking order – should follow that ruling, at least until a higher court says otherwise. After all, one intuitive way many of us understand a just set of rules is that they are applied to everyone who finds themself in the same situation in the same way. The principle of *stare decisis* lies at the heart of lawyerly arguments. It explains why lawyers cite and rely so significantly on the judgments of earlier cases as "precedents" when they seek to persuade judges to decide some matter in favour of their clients.

The second fundamental term, *ratio decidendi,* is closely related to *stare decisis*. The phrase *ratio decidendi* means "the reason for the decision." It is intended to refer to the precise principle or "rule" of law on which the outcome of a judicial decision depended. What legal principle *must* the judge have accepted to come to the particular decision they did? Because the reasons for judgment produced by judges in actual cases are often long, detailed, and heavily fact laden, much of the work of law students and litigation lawyers consists of poring assiduously through the text of a decision that is favourable to one's client, to seek to recite and apply it as though it were as definitive and non-contentious as the words of an Act of Parliament. But lawyers can and often do disagree about what the precise *ratio decidendi* (or *ratio,* for short) of any particular case might be. And therein lies the source of some legal argumentation and advocacy.

And so we come to the final of our three Latin phrases: *obiter dicta. Obiter dicta* means something like "incidental words." One may think as *obiter* statements in a judge's written reasons for judgment as rather like the antithesis of the *ratio. Obiter dicta* refers to language in a judicial decision that may, indeed, seem to reflect the judge's favoured view on some point of law, but unless it was necessary for the judge to actually decide that particular point of law to reach the decision in the specific case before them, then such comments form no binding part of the judgment for purposes of seeking to apply the case as precedent in future litigation. Once again, determining whether a particular comment on the law found in a judge's decision forms part of the (legally binding) *ratio* or is merely *obiter dicta* is not always a straightforward matter and can be a lively source of debate between lawyers in the courtroom and students in the law school classroom.

TN: *It sounds as though mastering these sorts of principles requires considerable experience beyond the law school classroom. So is the best way to start thinking like a lawyer to perhaps get some practical experience alongside law school course work? Maybe telling law school applicants they are going to learn to "think like lawyers" is more of an advertising claim by law schools than something they can realistically set as a goal for law school education.*

CN: Many law students share this very practical (and in some ways, rather skeptical) view. And sometimes their skepticism can emerge very early on in their law school career. Having laboured over some cases decided when their grandparents were toddlers involving legal principles encountered about as frequently by real-world lawyers as full solar eclipses, they understandably may start to think that it might be a good idea to seek some hands-on legal experience outside the classroom. In this view, they are often encouraged by worldly wise upper-year students. And so we do find many first-year students these days who are keen to dive into files at their law school's legal clinic or to participate in moot court competitions (on which more will be said in chapter 9) within weeks of arriving at law school for the first time. Through these more practical or applied activities, they hope to find a shorter path to the elusive goal of learning to think like a lawyer (and perhaps enhance their CVs in the process).

It may be an unfashionable or unpopular (perhaps even a heretical) view, but I have to say that I don't think this is always the best use of a first-year law student's scarce time, at least in the first term of their first year. The first-year law curriculum is a foundational experience, and law students benefit most from it if they immerse themselves wholeheartedly in it. There will be plenty of time in the upper years to participate in the variety of exciting extracurricular (or co-curricular) experiences that are part of an enriching law school experience.

TN: So whether the purpose of the first-year law program is to help students learn to "think like lawyers" or not, you are suggesting that it is still a unique learning experience and a valuable one, and that students should focus on their courses in first year rather than on extracurricular activities, even if those extracurricular activities might be more directly related to developing practical legal skills, like participating in moots or working at the law school clinic?

CN: That's my personal perspective. In short, it is not at all clear to me if "thinking like a lawyer," at least as many law professors interpret this phrase, always has very much to do with what most practising lawyers do in their day-to-day legal practice. Nor is it clear that law school is really well equipped to prepare (or necessarily interested in preparing) their graduates to think the way most practising lawyers actually have to think and work to build and sustain successful legal practices. But that isn't necessarily a weakness of law school. It may even be a strength. Perhaps a more realistic way to describe the mission of most university-affiliated law schools is that they help students

> learn how to practise "lawyering like a thinker" – that is, to engage thoughtfully, purposefully, reflectively, creatively, and intelligently in one's professional life, rather than to conduct one's professional practice merely by relying upon precedent forms or document templates, clichés, pat responses, and intuitive reactions. Instead of producing a stream of "paint-by-numbers" pictures, we would like to see lawyers inspired and dedicated to contributing thoughtful, creative, and socially useful works of the lawyer's art.

Conclusion

We have talked in this chapter about law school's broad educational goals and unique pedagogical methods in a very general, high-level way. In the next few chapters we will drill down a little more to look in closer detail at some of the specific features of the law school educational experience. We also want to examine (no pun intended) how law school evaluations – examinations and papers – are in some ways very similar to methods of evaluation seen in other faculties of the university but in a few ways are distinctly different.

Appendix C: A Simplified Example of the Socratic Method

We thought it might be helpful to provide, by way of illustration, a little sample of what the Socratic case method might look like in practice. So we have reproduced here a slightly edited version of a Socratic discussion of a very old contracts case from 1789, *Payne v Cave*. It actually would be quite unusual to discuss such an old case in a Canadian law school contracts class. But we have chosen this unusual case for a particular reason that we will reveal at the end of this little exercise.

Elsewhere in the book, TN generally poses the questions, which are printed in italics. In this appendix, we have switched places. In the Socratic classroom, it is the professor who poses the questions and the students that take centre stage; so in this appendix CN's questions appear in italics and TN's answers in bold roman font.

CN: The case we are considering is Payne v Cave. *Can you briefly state the facts of the case, as you understand them?*

TN: The plaintiff in the case had been the owner of something called a "worm-tub," which the plaintiff had put up for sale at an auction. The defendant was a bidder at that auction. The defendant bid £40 at the auction for the plaintiff's worm-tub. That was the highest bid. But the auctioneer believed that the bid was not high enough, so, after the defendant made his bid, the auctioneer "dwelt on the offer." He delayed bringing down his hammer.

The defendant asked him why he was delaying. The auctioneer answered by saying something about the weight of the item being sold, and why that justified a much

higher price than the defendant's bid. The defendant asked the auctioneer if he would "warrant" the weight of the item. The auctioneer said he would not. The defendant then rescinded his offer; so the item was not sold that day. Instead, the item was sold the next day, to the defendant, but for only £30. The plaintiff is now suing for £10 – the difference between the defendant's original high bid at the auction and the lower actual amount that the defendant eventually ended up paying.

CN: Will you give the plaintiff's argument?

TN: The plaintiff's claim is that the defendant should still have to honour the full amount of his original high bid. When you place a bid, you must be prepared to honour it. Otherwise, it would be unfair to the seller, because the moment you make a bid you void the next highest bid.

CN: Do you agree with that?

TN: No. I agree with what the court decided.

CN: Let's come to that now, then. What did the court decide?

TN: The court decided in favour of the defendant. The plaintiff was not entitled to the extra £10 he was suing for.

CN: Can you suggest a reason?

TN: The court decided that holding the defendant to the bid would create an unfair agreement between the bidder and the auctioneer. The bidder would be bound by the bid he had made, but the auctioneer would not be bound to accept it. So it was decided that a bid does not have to be honoured unless the hammer has come down and the auctioneer declares the item to be sold. Otherwise, it seems one sided and unfair if you hold the bidder to their bid but the auctioneer is given time to look for a better offer. It seems to

give the auctioneer an unfair advantage to be able to keep looking for a chance to get more money while still having the safety of knowing that, if no higher bid materializes, the item has been sold.

CN: *But isn't that exactly what an auction is all about? Doesn't everyone who comes to an auction understand that the auctioneer's job is to get the highest possible price? Isn't that part of the context in which people make bids at an auction? If bidders are free to withdraw their bids when they see no one else is prepared to bid more, isn't there a risk that people might come to auctions and place phony bids just to "bid up" the price of items, with no real intention of ever buying? If there is no risk in placing those sorts of stalking bids – if they can always be withdrawn with no consequences – wouldn't that make conducting fair auctions impossible?*

TN: I would still argue that the decision of the court was fair. The auctioneer *could* have easily held the defendant to his bid of £40. He just had to bring the hammer down. But he didn't. He wavered and said, "this it not a high enough offer," and continued to wait, hoping that another bid would be made. This entire case began just because the auctioneer waited and claimed that £40 was not a high enough bid.

CN: *How long should an auctioneer have to accept a bid before we say that he is delaying? Ten seconds? Five? Four point seven? Where do we draw the line?*

TN: I don't think it can be a specific number of seconds. How about a time that is reasonable under all the circumstances?

CN: *How would you define a "reasonable time"? What is reasonable for one person might be unreasonable to another, wouldn't it?*

TN: How about, reasonable for an auction like this one? I haven't been to any auctions myself, but I assume there are rules or customs that people who do go to auctions understand. Having seen auctions on TV, it seems to me that the auctioneer usually counts, "Going once, going twice, sold." So perhaps there has to be a clear counting system like that: a clear time that has been set out that both the auctioneer and all the bidders are clearly in agreement with. For example, once the count begins, it will be clear that the bidder knows that once the auctioneer reaches the end, brings down his hammer and says "sold," they will be held to their bid. And the same rule applies to the auctioneer. Once they have brought the hammer down and said "sold," they understand the bid will be honoured. But up until then, they know there is a risk that a bidder may take back their bid.

CN: So what's reasonable will depend on the circumstances and customs of the auction?

TN: Yes. That seems fair to me.

CN: Now, the plaintiff made an argument to the effect that before the defendant made his bid at £40, another bidder had placed a bid that was lower than £40 but was still higher (maybe significantly higher) than £30. But £30 was the price the defendant eventually paid the next day for the worm-tub. The plaintiff argued that it was unfair that the defendant could basically void that earlier bid (which was for a higher amount than the plaintiff ultimately received as payment for his item) by making a bid that perhaps he never really intended to honour. What do you think of that argument?

TN: I don't think it applies at all in this case. The whole reason the auctioneer delayed bringing down the hammer was that he thought £40 was too low a price for the item. So, in no circumstance does it seem that he would have accepted an even lower bid on that day. He would have been just as unhappy – even more unhappy – with that bid as well. To me, it seems as if the plaintiff and the auctioneer can't have their cake and eat it, too. The only reason the defendant rescinded his offer was that the auctioneer waited too long to accept his bid. So it seems almost silly to claim that the £40 offer eliminated some other offer that might have been higher than the £30 price they ended up with the next day. This whole case only came about because the auctioneer didn't accept the £40 offer right away.

The plaintiff could have chosen to try to sell the item at a set price at market. He chose instead to sell it by auction in an attempt to get more money. So, if you want to sell by auction, you have to accept the rules and the risks of an auction. That includes the risk that a bidder might rescind an offer before the auctioneer says "sold."

CN: So, in sum, when a person goes to an auction and makes a bid at a certain price, he is not actually expected to honour that bid? He can simply withdraw it?

TN: No. He can only withdraw it if the auctioneer has not yet accepted the bid in an appropriate time and manner.

CN: And, please remind me, how do you determine the appropriate time and manner?

TN: You determine that based on the normal or reasonable circumstances of an auction.

CN: How should we characterize what the bidder is doing legally? Are they making an offer to buy? Or are they accepting an offer to sell? How can we characterize what happens at an auction bid in contractual terms, do you think?

TN: I think the bidder is making an offer to buy the item. But the offer wouldn't become a contract until the auctioneer accepts the offer to buy.

CN: So you wouldn't be prepared to say that the auctioneer is making an offer to sell that is accepted by the bidder, perhaps subject to some condition?

TN: I don't think so.

CN: Why not?

TN: I don't think it becomes a contract until the auctioneer accepts the offer.

CN: Can you suggest a reason for this?

TN: You would need a price. And the auctioneer isn't offering to sell at any particular price. The auctioneer is sort of putting out an invitation for bidders to make offers, but the auctioneer doesn't name a price, so there wouldn't really be an offer to sell that anyone could accept yet.

CN: Let's recap your argument. You have now articulated a legal rule: that, at an auction, a bidder can withdraw their bid at any time before the auctioneer has accepted it in an appropriate time and manner based on the normal or reasonable circumstances of an auction, such as by bringing down the hammer and saying "sold."

TN: Yes, that would be my rule, and I think that is what the court decided as well.

CN: You've also explained why, in your opinion, this rule seems just, based on your understanding of the particular facts and circumstances of the case.

Now, today in Canada, to find the law that would govern the sort of dispute that occurred in the Payne v Cave *case, we don't look to the common law anymore. We look to a statute. Every province and territory in Canada has sale of goods legislation that includes a provision that deals with sales at auction.*[26] *They are all basically identical. Here, for example, is what the Ontario* Sale of Goods Act *says:*

> **56** In case of a sale by auction,
>
> . . .
>
> (b) a sale is complete when the auctioneer announces its completion by the fall of a hammer or in any other customary manner, and until such announcement is made any bidder may retract his, her or its bid.

That law is very close to the rule you've stated as the appropriate rule based on your analysis of Payne v Cave.

If the goal of law school was simply to learn a collection of rules, it would have been much simpler to have asked you to read that one very short section of the Sale of Goods Act, *wouldn't it? You would immediately have had the correct "answer" as to when a bidder at an auction can and cannot withdraw a bid. That would certainly have been a lot quicker. Perhaps it would have been more efficient, too. But defenders of the Socratic method would argue that by asking you instead*

---

26 *Sale of Goods Act* (BC), RSBC 1996, c 410, s 72(b); *Sale of Goods Act* (AB), RSA 2000, c S-2, s 57(b); *The Sale of Goods Act* (SK), RSS 1978, c S-1, s 57(b); *The Sale of Goods Act* (MB), CCSM c S10, s 59(b); *Sale of Goods Act* (ON), RSO 1990, c S.1, s 56(b); *Sale of Goods Act* (NB), RSNB 2016, c 110, s 74(b); *Sale of Goods Act* (NS), RSNS 1989, c 408, s 59(b); *Sale of Goods Act* (NL), RSNL 1990, c S-6, s 59(b); *Sale of Goods Act* (YK), RSY 2002, c 198, s 55(2); *Sale of Goods Act* (NWT/Nu), RSNWT 1988, c S-2, s 65(2).

to read a case and be prepared to discuss the principles articulated in that case as you understand them, you have a chance to develop a much better and deeper understanding not only of one idiosyncratic rule about bids at auctions, but also of some of the general principles that underlie that rule and the reasoning process on which the formulation of the rule is based. The purpose of reading a case like this, then, is not just to give you an example of a particular legal rule that you should dutifully write down and memorize in the unlikely event that you one day have a client who runs into a similar problem at an auction. It is to try to understand the reasoning process: Why is it that the law allows a bidder at an auction to rescind a bid until the moment the auctioneer brings down the hammer? What does this help us understand, more generally, about the elements of a binding contract?

By the way, this is completely irrelevant to the legal principle in the case, but just out of interest, what was the item they were selling in Payne v Cave*?*

TN: A "worm-tub"?

CN: Exactly. Do you know what a worm-tub is?

TN: No.

CN: A worm-tub is apparently a very large tub that is used as a condenser in the distillery business. The "worm" refers to a coil, made of copper or perhaps of pewter, as in this case. The distilled vapour runs through this coil while it is immersed in water in the worm-tub. The water cools the coil, and the vapour in the coil then condenses back to liquid. This, apparently, was a traditional method of making whiskey that was common prior to the mid-nineteenth century, and may still be used in at least a few distilleries in the UK today. These condensing worm-tubs were very large, apparently, and quite expensive. It's hard to be sure what £40 in 1789 would be worth today, but it would certainly be many thousands of pounds.

TN: And using the Socratic method sounds like a way to condense the key facts and distill the key legal principles. Am I thinking like a lawyer or like a distiller? You be the judge.

CN: There is one final note I would like to make. I mentioned at the beginning of this little exercise that I had a particular reason for choosing Payne v Cave *for our simplified Socratic/case method example. The reason I chose this antiquated case for our illustration is that* Payne v Cave *was evidently the very first case used by Christopher Columbus Langdell himself when he first introduced his new case method at the Harvard Law School in 1870. And the first few questions I asked you about the case included the same questions Langdell asked students in that very first class all those years ago.*[27]

TN: I don't imagine any of them knew what a worm-tub was, either.[28]

---

27 See Samuel F Batchelder, "Christopher C Langdell" (1906) 18:8 Green Bag 437.

28 One final note: The auctioneer's hammer is, of course, often called a gavel. The gavel is frequently used as a symbol of law and justice – including on the cover of this book. However, although gavels may be used by American judges and are regularly depicted in television and film courtroom scenes, Canadian judges do not use gavels, nor were they traditionally used in UK courts, either. The fact that the gavel has neverthless become such a ubiquitous symbol of the law even in countries where judges do not use them is a testament to the remarkable influence of American popular entertainment. (Cynics have sometimes unfairly remarked that the gavel is used by American judges to remind everyone that justice too often goes to whoever can afford to pay the highest price.)

7

the role of statute law: interpretation acts and acts of interpretation

Introduction

We have talked a great deal in this book about the influence of Christopher Columbus Langdell on North American legal education. When Langdell introduced the "case method" at the Harvard Law School, "case law" (that is, the common law) was the principal source of the law in the United States, Canada, and the United Kingdom. It was in the courts that the common law had developed over time. The common law school curriculum, particularly in the first year, continues in many ways to reflect the glory of the common law, with its emphasis on courses such as contracts, torts, and property. The fundamental principles of all of these fields of law evolved in the courts, not the legislatures. Law students, then, can surely be forgiven for thinking that it is the pronouncements of judges, and judges alone, that are authoritative.

But beginning sometime in the twentieth century, the role of legislation – including subordinate legislation such as regulations and rules – began to assume ever increasing importance in Canada, the United Kingdom, the United States, and elsewhere. Of course, legislatures had not been asleep since the Norman Conquest. Statutes had been enacted for centuries. But for the past 100 years or so the volume and scope of legislation and regulation have increased vastly. The impact of this proliferation of statutes and related regulations and rules is now reflected in the law school curriculum, too, although principally in upper-year courses. Many (some would argue most) substantive law upper-year courses deal with areas of law in which statutes, rather than the common law, play a dominant role. The role of the courts in these areas of the law is also crucial, but it is of a somewhat different nature. It falls to the courts to interpret and apply the statutory language that has been enacted by Parliament and the provincial legislatures. As statutes have become more important to the daily work of the lawyer, the art of statutory interpretation has become a subject of growing importance and growing interest for lawyers and law students.

Scholars in many disciplines, such as theology and philosophy, are familiar with the field of "hermeneutics," which deals with the principles of interpretation of texts. Hermeneutics has thus sometimes been dubbed the "philosophy of interpretation."[1] The erudite principles of hermeneutics are sometimes alluded to by learned jurisprudential scholars. But in the ordinary day-to-day work of lawyers and judges, interpreting

1 See *Stanford Encyclopedia of Philosophy*, q.v. "hermeneutics."

statutory language involves less exotic and more practical and important approaches that can sometimes prove to be surprisingly difficult and controversial.

How Does Language Mean?

TN: This may be a silly question, but how can interpreting something like a statute be complicated? Wouldn't it be the whole point of a statute to make things clear, definite, and easy to understand? Shouldn't people have a right to expect that they can understand laws they are required to obey?

CN: Yet, we see ambiguity in language everywhere. Consider, for a moment, how we should interpret the following (actual) street sign:

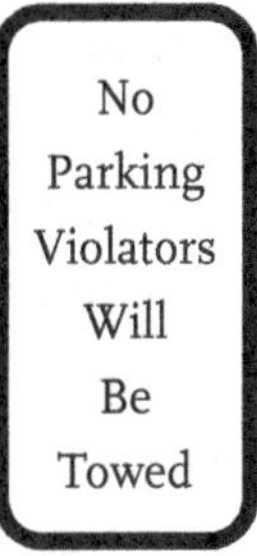

Since the sign includes no punctuation at all, it can be read in a number of different ways. In particular, the words on the sign, read literally, could mean (at least) two different things:

1. None of the people who violate the parking rules will be towed.
2. No parking is allowed here. Everyone who violates this warning will be towed.

TN: Actually, number one never even occurred to me . . .

CN: I'm guessing that's because your mind skipped past the ambiguity of the words themselves and went straight to a sensible interpretation: A meaning that you probably expected from a "no parking" sign and that avoids an apparent absurdity. I would think that most reasonable people would agree with you that meaning number 2 must be what the authorities who posted the sign had in mind. After all, there wouldn't be any obvious reason for someone to put up a sign telling drivers they need not ever worry about having their cars towed even if they are violating the "no parking" rules.

But note that to arrive at this sensibly "correct" interpretation, just reading the words entirely on their own and absent any context is not enough – even though none of the words is unusual or technical, and even though the entire sign consists of only six words altogether. You must go beyond simply reading the words to determine the most likely *purpose* of the sign. That, in turn, requires some consideration of the context in which the sign is being used, your guess about what mischief the sign poster is trying to stop, your experience with similar signs, and so on. The words themselves – because of the missing punctuation – are ambiguous.

In fact, someone might argue that they are worse than just ambiguous. If this sign is read as a single sentence, for instance, it really *can't* be interpreted under conventional rules of English grammar and syntax as a restriction on parking and an accompanying warning about being towed if you ignore that restriction. The "correct" interpretation, therefore, requires us to insert a period after the word "parking" that isn't actually there.

The ambiguity of this simple parking sign is a simple illustration of a much more complex (and significant) set of interpretation challenges that confront courts every day. When the words of a statute, on their own, allow for more than one meaning, disputes may well arise between people who will be affected differently by the statute depending on which of those alternative meanings is the "correct" one.

TN: This example reminds me of the famous six-word story attributed (though some argue incorrectly)[2] *to Ernest Hemingway: "For Sale: Baby Shoes. Never worn." The story that might lie behind these six words is up for personal interpretation. In fact, it's more than interpretation. The reader really has to create meaning for themselves.*

The Role of Intention

CN: In the case of the Hemingway (or pseudo-Hemingway) example, the literal meaning of the words is clear. The uncertainty – indeed, the mystery or perhaps the tragedy – lies in the untold story implied by this simple six-word classified ad. It is unlikely that the writer of this ergodic "micro novel" had one specific underlying narrative in mind. Leaving it to the readers to create the explanation for themselves seems to very much be what the writer intended. It doesn't

2 See Frederick A Wright, "The Short Story Just Got Shorter: Hemingway, Narrative, and the Six-Word Urban Legend" (2014) 47:2 J of Pop Cul 327.

matter if different readers imagine different backstories. In fact, that is probably the very point.

But with legislation, it is expected to apply in the same way to all. We are all equal under the law. When the language seems to allow for more than one meaning, how do we discern the "correct" interpretation? Now, one might think it makes perfect sense to try to figure out what the original drafters of legislation "intended." And that, we might suppose, is the correct way of interpreting an otherwise ambiguous statute. But while it is certainly essential to determine the legislative purpose of a statute, that is often much easier said than done. First of all, how, exactly, does one go about determining what the original intention of Parliament (or a provincial legislature) was when it enacted a statute? Parliament, after all, isn't a person. How do you determine the "intention" of a collective body? Perhaps we might go through Hansard and see just what was said about the legislation by the representatives of the government when it introduced the bill that was later passed into law. Or perhaps we might review all of the explanations offered during debates over the bill. In some cases, looking at the history of the legislation might be useful. But the problem with looking to statements by government ministers or other MPs as proof of the original intention of a piece of legislation is that we run the risk of substituting the words spoken by a member of the government or other member of Parliament for the words of the statute itself. And that doesn't seem right.

Let's take a silly, exaggerated example. Suppose Parliament were to enact a statute making it a crime to bring a dog into the waiting area of any hospital emergency room.

Now suppose someone were to bring their cat into a hospital emergency room. Can this person be charged under the statute? Obviously, a cat is not a dog. But now suppose that, when the legislation was introduced into Parliament, the minister responsible explained:

> Although the bill uses the word "dog," it is not to be interpreted literally since, of course, the law will extend to cats as well. That is what the bill means, and that is how it must be correctly understood.

Does that solve the matter? The word "dog" in this statute was apparently *intended* by the very people who drafted the statute to mean "cats" as well. If that's correct, then the person who brought their cat into the emergency room can be charged and convicted. Does that seem fair to you?[3] Now, it might well be the case that the person who brought their cat to the waiting room wasn't even aware of this law. They may not have even known, in other words, that there was a law that said it was a crime to bring a "dog" into a hospital emergency room (let alone that such a law was supposedly intended by its drafters to include cats) That fact, by itself,

3 In a case decided by the Supreme Court of Canada in 2025, *Telus Communications Inc. v Federation of Canadian Municipalities*, 2025 SCC 15, at para 35, the majority judgment reproduced a quote by Lord Bingham from an earlier UK House of Lords decision, *R. (Quintavalle) v. Secretary of State for Health*, [2003] UKHL 13, [2003] 2 A.C. 687, at para. 9 that referred to a similar "dogs vs cats" interpretation question:

> There is, I think, no inconsistency between the rule that statutory language retains the meaning it had when Parliament used it and the rule that a statute is always speaking. If Parliament, however long ago, passed an Act applicable to dogs, it could not properly be interpreted to apply to cats; but it could properly be held to apply to animals which were not regarded as dogs when the Act was passed but are so regarded now.

wouldn't assist the cat owner. There is a fundamental principle in Canadian law that "ignorance of the law is no excuse." If you prefer a fancier Latin phrase for this principle it is this: *Ignorantia legis neminem excusat*. So if the cat owner had instead brought a dog (a pet that barks rather than meows) to the emergency room, the fact that they were unaware that they had broken the law wouldn't save them from prosecution.

Now, if you read the short discussion of criminal law back in chapter 5 carefully, you might be wondering why our cat owner in this example couldn't simply argue that they should be acquitted even if the statute does apply to cats because they had no *mens rea* – no "guilty mind." The cat owner didn't know about this law, so they genuinely didn't think they were doing anything wrong. But mistakenly thinking you were doing something "innocently" because you didn't realize it was a crime is not what we mean by a lack of *mens rea*. You will be said to have *mens rea* as long as you intended to commit the act that happens to be prohibited by law. The fact that you genuinely didn't know that the act you intentionally committed *was* prohibited by law doesn't make any difference. There is a weighty Latin phrase for this principle too – "*Ignorantia juris non excusat*": ignorance of the law is no excuse. In other words, if you knowingly brought a dog into the emergency room, not realizing there was a law against doing so, you have still committed the crime. You brought in the dog – that is the *actus reus*. And you intended to bring in the dog. You therefore had the necessary *mens rea* to be convicted, even though you were not knowingly breaking the law.

On the other hand, let's suppose you came into the emergency room carrying your backpack but, unbeknownst to you, a small dog had managed to sneak into your backpack without your knowledge just before you arrived. Now you may successfully argue you had no *mens rea*. In this case, you did not *intend* to bring a dog into the room at all – you didn't even realize you had done so. But the reason you may escape prosecution is that you did not intend to commit the specific act (bringing a dog into an emergency room) that was prohibited by law. Whether you did or didn't happen to know that bringing a dog into an emergency room was illegal is irrelevant. (At least it is irrelevant in determining your guilt, as opposed, perhaps, to determining the appropriate sentence for your "crime.")

TN: But I would argue that the statute is clear. It uses the word "dog." I mean, there is a broader term that could have been used by the drafters: for example, "pets." Isn't that correct?

CN: That is both sensible and reasonable, it seems to me. But let's return now to the plight of our cat owner facing imminent arrest for bringing their cat into the hospital emergency room by law enforcement officers seeking to enforce the statute based, let us suppose, on their understanding of what the drafters had originally intended. Now, let's change our facts a little and suppose that the cat owner *was* aware of the law they are being accused of breaking. They had, perhaps, been reading a copy of that very law just before they had to be rushed to the emergency room. The cat owner knew that certain pets were prohibited. But they also knew that the statute specifically used the word "dog," not "cat." How could they reasonably have known that the word "dog" was intended to have some special meaning in the context of this particular statute? In a democratic society, surely citizens have a right to be able to assume that they can rely that the words used by Parliament will normally have their plain and ordinary meaning. So the suggestion that the "intention" of Parliament should govern interpretation (if, that is, "intention" means something other than the objective intention to be determined based on the words in the context in which they are used in the statute) certainly must not be the universal rule.

There is another problem, too. How can we ever really say what Parliament's "intention" was beyond looking to the words that were chosen for the statute itself? The minister placing the bill before Parliament may well, in their own mind, have "intended" for the word "dog" to include "cat." But one minister – even a minister in a government that enjoys a majority of seats in the House of Commons – does not, and cannot, speak for Parliament itself. We have no idea what each and every member of the House of Commons or the Senate had in mind when they voted on the bill or what the governor general took the words to mean when she gave the bill royal assent. Surely at least some of these people (and probably all or most of them) took the statute to mean precisely what it said: It applied to dogs, not cats. We certainly want to know the intention of the legislature, but that isn't necessarily the subjective intention of any individual legislator.

TN: *And I know for a fact that if the members of Parliament who voted to pass the bill were "cat people," they definitely only meant dogs in that statute. Trust me.*

The "Persons" Case

CN: This silly "dogs" and "cats" example is, of course, entirely fictional. But there are real-life examples where drafters' presumed original "intent" does clash with the ordinary apparent meaning of a word under circumstances where much more is at stake than determining which sort of furry pet you are permitted to have with you in a hospital waiting room.

Perhaps the most famous and notorious example in Canadian history occurred in the 1929 case of *Edwards v Attorney-General of Canada*,[4] which is sometimes today referred to as the "persons" case. The *Edwards* case was a decision of the Judicial Committee of the Privy Council in the UK. The Judicial Committee of the Privy Council (the Privy Council) was a special appeal tribunal. As a practical matter, its members usually consisted of so-called Lords of Appeal – that is, the judges of the House of Lords, the highest appellate court in the United Kingdom, which is today the UK Supreme Court.

In those days, it may surprise you to learn, the Privy Council functioned as the final court of appeal for Canada. The Supreme Court of Canada was not actually, for many years, the "supreme" court for Canadian legal decisions. Decisions of the Supreme Court of Canada could be appealed to the Privy Council. That is no longer true, of course. Appeals of Supreme Court of Canada decisions

4 [1930] AC 124.

to the Privy Council ended, in the case of civil matters (like contracts, torts, and property law), in 1949 and in the case of criminal law matters in 1933. But the *Edwards* case was decided at a time when the Privy Council was still, in effect, the highest court of appeal for Canadian cases.

The *Edwards* case began as a reference to the Supreme Court of Canada in 1928. The question that had been referred to the Supreme Court to decide was this:

> Does the word "Persons" in section 24 of the *British North America Act, 1867*, include female persons?

It seems shocking today that such a question could ever have been in doubt. Of course women are persons. Who would ever have suggested otherwise? The context in which this question was posed to the court helps explain why, back in 1928, some people thought the court needed to opine on the question. The real issue that was being debated was not whether, as a grammatical matter, the word "persons" included women. The real issue was whether or not women were qualified to be appointed to the Senate of Canada. At the time the *British North America Act, 1867* was drafted, women were not eligible to vote in Canada. So, some people reasoned, the intention of the drafters must have been not to permit women to sit in the Senate, either.

Now, as it happened, most Canadian men would not have been eligible to be appointed to the Senate at the time of Confederation either, because one of the qualifications was that a senator must own property worth at least $4,000. That would have been a significant amount of money in 1867. We know, for example, that the average daily wage of a carpenter in Toronto in 1870 was about $1.75.[5] So $4,000 would represent about nine years of income for such a person. In short, only a very small number of fairly wealthy people (whether male or female) were eligible for Senate seats in 1867.

As outrageous as it may seem today, in response to the reference question the Supreme Court of Canada decided that women would not be included as eligible persons to be appointed to the Senate within the meaning of the *British North America Act*. An important part of the justification offered by Chief Justice Anglin, who wrote the majority decision, was based on the presumed intention of the legislature at the time the Act was passed, with particular emphasis placed on the meaning of the word "qualified" in light of the context of the common law and consistent practice from 1867.

The Supreme Court of Canada's decision was overturned by the Privy Council. And the judgment of Lord Sankey, on behalf of the Privy Council, contains a passage that has since become very famous among Canadian constitutional law scholars:

> The *British North America Act* planted in Canada a living tree capable of growth and expansion within its natural limits. The object of the Act was to grant a Constitution to Canada. Like all written constitutions it has been subject to development through usage and convention.[6]

---

5 JG Snell, "The Cost of Living in Canada in 1870" (1979) 12:23 Soc His 186.

6 *Re Section 24 of the BNA Act*, [1930] 1 DLR 98 at 106-7 (UK JCPC) (per Lord Sankey, LC)

The meaning of words, then, at least in constitutional documents, need not be fixed. It may evolve over time. This view has many strong supporters, but also fierce opponents – including the adherents of originalism, of whom the late US Supreme Court Justice Antonin Scalia was an especially influential example.

Interpreting constitutional documents, needless to say, might well involve different principles and different goals than interpreting the language of ordinary statutes. The only point to be made here is that when interpreting statutes, the search for the underlying "purpose" of the legislation involves more than simply a search for the supposed subjective "intention" of the drafters, as we will see in our discussion of the "Modern Approach" to statutory interpretation below.

Latin Maxims (Canons of Construction)

CN: Many first-year law students come to class expecting to learn some rules. We all like certainty. It is understandably more satisfying to be able to declare that some disputed matter may be solved by the application of a certain rule, rather than to have to resort to some equivocating "weasel words" like "It depends . . ."

TN: That's how you can spot a lawyer. Ask them anything, and they will always respond with "It depends," or "This isn't legal advice, but . . ."

CN: Sadly, the only apt response to many legal questions will have to be "it depends." In the realm of statutory interpretation, the courts developed a number of general interpretive approaches that came to be encapsulated in pithy maxims.

Best of all, these maxims are in Latin so that even when they aren't particularly useful, they can help you sound very learned and profound.

Here are a couple of simple examples.

Ejusdem generis

Ejusdem generis means "of the same kind." The *ejusdem generis* "rule" is a maxim (or "canon") of statutory interpretation that says that when a statute contains a list of items including a number of specifically enumerated terms, followed by general words, you should limit the application of those general words to things of the same sort as the specifically listed terms. For example, suppose a hypothetical statute said:

> No person may operate a truck, automobile, tractor, or other vehicle anywhere in the province without an operator's permit issued by the Minister of Transportation.

Would a bicycle be considered an "other vehicle"? In many other circumstances, a bicycle is considered a "vehicle." Would this statute require everyone who wished to ride a bicycle to obtain an operator's permit? Applying the *ejusdem generis* rule, we might say that even though the statute uses the broad phrase "other vehicle," we must interpret that phrase in the context of the specific examples of vehicles that precede it: truck, automobile, and tractor. All of those vehicles share one important common element: they are motor powered. An ordinary bicycle is not a vehicle "of the same kind" and therefore, we might conclude, the legislation does not apply to a bicycle rider.

TN: I can see why that example is tricky, though. When a bicycle is on the road it is acting as a vehicle. I don't know if I would be opposed to requiring a licence for bicyclists if they want to ride on the road. I mean, well . . . it depends.

Expressio unius est exclusio alterius

CN: This phrase means that express reference to one thing excludes another. Consider this example. Suppose a hypothetical statute reads as follows:

> An airline may deny boarding to any passenger wearing a red tie.

Now, notice the statute does not specifically say whether or not airlines can deny boarding to passengers on any other basis. Could the airline deny boarding to a passenger with an orange tie? You may also observe that the statute does not specifically say that passengers may be denied boarding *only* if they are wearing red ties. And the statute says nothing at all about passengers with orange ties. But one might assume that the legislator's decision to specifically include a reference to red ties excludes the application of the statute to passengers with ties of any different colour.

The Modern Approach

There are many more of these little Latin "canons of construction." They aren't rules of law. Courts are not bound by them. At most they are occasionally helpful, sometimes reasonable guidelines that might assist courts in deciding how to interpret statutory language subject to a careful consideration of all the facts and circumstances.

Canadian courts today are not always impressed by Latin maxims and refer to a more holistic "modern" approach to statutory interpretation which seeks to determine the meaning of a statute by reference to its text, context and purpose.[7] Let's consider how that might work, taking an example from a well-known Supreme Court of Canada case, *Rizzo & Rizzo Shoes Ltd (Re)*.[8]

TN: We might be using the term "well known" a little liberally there . . .

CN: The statute that the court had to interpret in this case was Ontario's *Employment Standards Act*. That statute (as it was worded at the time) provided that where the employment of an employee is terminated *by the employer* without giving the employee a specifically prescribed period of notice, "the employer shall pay termination pay in an amount equal to the wages that the employee would have been entitled to receive . . . for the period of notice prescribed."

In this case, the employer had been petitioned into bankruptcy by its creditors. As a result of the bankruptcy, the employees' employment had been terminated. Were these employees entitled to severance, termination, or vacation pay under the *Employment Standards Act*?

On the one hand, it could be argued that the employees were not terminated "by the employer." They were

7 See *Telus Communications Inc. v Federation of Canadian Municipalities*, above, note 3 and para 30.

8 [1998] 1 SCR 27.

terminated by the bankruptcy. That was how the Ontario Court of Appeal interpreted the statute when it denied that the terminated employees were entitled to claim amounts for severance pay and termination pay under the statute. On the other hand, perhaps the statute was only intended to deny severance pay and termination pay when employees voluntarily left their own employment. That was the reading favoured by the terminated employees.

The former employees appealed the Ontario Court of Appeal's decision to the Supreme Court of Canada. The Supreme Court of Canada overturned the decision of the Court of Appeal. The Supreme Court of Canada disagreed with the way in which the Ontario Court of Appeal had interpreted the *Employment Standards Act*. The Supreme Court conceded that "the plain meaning of the words of the provisions here in question appears to restrict the obligation to pay termination and severance pay to those employers who have actively terminated the employment of their employees. At first blush, bankruptcy does not fit comfortably into this interpretation."[9] However, this analysis, in the court's view, was incomplete. The words of the Act "must be read in their entire context and in their grammatical and ordinary sense harmoniously with the scheme of the Act, the object of the Act, and the intention of Parliament."[10]

Interpreting the language in this broader, purposive way (i.e., "harmoniously with the scheme of the Act"), the Supreme Court notes that the effect of the Court of Appeal's

9 *Ibid* at para 20.

10 *Ibid* at para 21, citing Elmer Dreidger, *Construction of Statutes*, 2nd ed (Toronto: Butterworths, 1983) at 87.

decision seemed arbitrary and unfair. For example, it would mean that an employee terminated by an employer just one day before bankruptcy would be entitled to claim severance and termination pay while an employee terminated one day later by the bankruptcy itself would be entitled to nothing. The Supreme Court concluded that "'terminated by the employer' must be interpreted to include termination resulting from the bankruptcy of the employer."[11] Do you agree?

TN: Hmm. I'm going to have to get back to you on that question. Maybe after studying the law for about three years, give or take.

CN: Let's return now, briefly, to our "No Parking Violators" sign. Whatever alternative meanings the words of that sign might bear as a technical, grammatical matter, it seems, after all, that your preferred interpretation is the most reasonable way to understand the words "read in their entire context and in their grammatical and ordinary sense harmoniously with the scheme of the [sign] and the object the [sign]. And your interpretation also avoids interpreting the sign to mean that parking violators will NEVER be towed, which would be "absurd or otherwise unacceptable" and therefore, under the modern approach, would be "presumed not to have been intended."[12]

TN: I'm glad to hear that. I did have one other observation to make about the sign. But for now, I think I will park that comment.

---

11 Above note 8 at para 40.

12 See *Telus Communications Inc. v Federation of Canadian Municipalities*, above, note 3 at para 76.

8

the dreaded final exam, the bell curve, class averages, and why you don't need to outrun the bear

Introduction: Grades Matter. So, What's the Matter with Grades?

Let's face it. Grades matter. They matter to students. They matter to employers. They matter to university admissions officers. They sometimes even matter to parents, grandparents, legal guardians, and sports team coaches. Like it or not, grades are the educational currency. You want to earn better grades. You sometimes try to negotiate for a raise in your grades. High grades are used as a measure of success. Low grades may be a sign that you may have to be let go.

With so much turning on grades, I thought it was important to find out more about how grades, grading, and evaluation generally work at law school.

Law School Evaluation: The Dreaded Final Exam

I was surprised and even a little disappointed to learn that final examinations still exist and continue to play a big part in law school evaluation. For many courses, 100 percent final examinations are still used. The idea of a 100 percent final exam makes me sick. So if you're like me, I should probably warn you that at least some and perhaps many of your law school grades will be based either entirely or mainly on final exams.

This fact can come as quite a shock. I can't speak to everyone's undergrad experience, but throughout my four years at the University of Toronto, I never had a single 100 percent final exam. I think the biggest final exam I ever wrote counted for no more than 30 percent of my final grade. Do I personally agree with this "all-your-eggs-in-one-basket" form of evaluation? No. I do not think a one-time examination is a fair assessment of skill and knowledge. How can everything you have learned in a year or even in one semester or term be properly tested in a couple of hours on a single day? The 100 percent final exam seems to me to be an out-of-date, unimaginative, even lazy way of evaluating adults studying complex and demanding university subjects. More importantly, it seems likely to be inaccurate, unnecessarily stressful,[1] and potentially quite unfair.

1 And law students really are under a lot of stress, even compared with students in other graduate and professional school programs, including medical students. Todd David Peterson and Elizabeth Waters Peterson, for example, have reported that "One study found that 44% of law students meet the criteria for clinically significant levels of psychological distress . . . Moreover, these problems seem unique to law students and are not generalizable to other overworked populations of graduate students. For instance, one study showed that compared to medical students in a similarly demanding academic situation, law students have significantly

But that is obviously not the view of most law schools and many Canadian law school professors. What do they know that I don't? Why do so many law professors still rely so heavily on one-off final exams? We'll come to that a little later. For now, it doesn't really matter what I may think about the deficiencies of final exams. What matters is knowing how they actually fit into the overall scheme of evaluation at most Canadian common law schools.

Different Types of Evaluations

Though final exams still loom large at Canadian law schools, there are a number of different ways that law school courses can be evaluated. Some of them can be very creative. Some of them look pretty similar to the evaluation methods used in typical undergraduate degree programs. Some of the most common law school course evaluation methods include the following:

1. 100 percent final "sit-down," open-book exam
2. 100 percent final take-home exam (There are several different variations of take-home exams. For example, you might be given 24 hours or 48 hours or even a few days to complete the exam, or you might be required to complete the exam within a two-, three-, or four-hour "block," but with the flexibility to select for yourself your preferred block of time on your preferred date within some given

higher levels of stress, stress symptoms, and alcohol abuse." Todd David Peterson & Elizabeth Waters Peterson, "Stemming the Tide of Law Student Depression: What Law Schools Need to Learn from the Science of Positive Psychology" (2009) 9:2 Yale J Health Pol'y L & Ethics 357 at 359.

range of days. Law schools use software programs that allow them to track exactly when you start and stop exams. And, with take-home exams, you might also expect the professor to impose strictly enforced word limits.)

3. 100 percent final "sit-down" closed-book exam. (Closed book exams do not seem to be very common in law school. But I understand that some law professors do still use them. We discuss that a little further below.)
4. 100 percent essay assignment
5. Various combinations of class participation, optional (or mandatory) writing assignments; optional (or mandatory) midterm tests or quizzes; optional (or mandatory) oral presentations, moots, or group assignments; and optional (or mandatory) creative assignments of various types. However, except for (usually smaller seminar-style) courses that are specifically designated as essay courses, it seems that most law school courses still include a final exam as at least one major component of course evaluation, even if it doesn't count for 100 percent of the course grade.

TN: *I know that final examinations still play a big role in law school evaluation. I have some objections to that that I will raise in a moment. But I also understand that other methods of evaluation, including those listed above, are used, too. How common are those other methods? What is the approximate "mix" of exams and other types of assignments that a law student can expect?*

CN: Each professor you have in law school, at least after the first year, will decide on the evaluation methods they wish to use for their own courses. Sometimes, in first-year courses, there may be a little more institutional standardization of evaluation methods at each law school intended to achieve some measure of consistency.

First-year students at most Canadian law schools take all or mostly the same courses. They don't get to choose their first-year courses or their first-year professors. They are more or less randomly assigned to different "sections" of courses, and each section is likely taught by a different professor. So Student A and Student B may both have taken first-year torts at the same law school in the same year, but they won't necessarily have been in the same torts class. Many law schools have decided that in the interests of fairness and consistency, it makes sense to try to make the first-year program as uniform as possible.

One way to achieve a little more consistency is by requiring similar evaluation methods for everyone. After the first year, achieving this kind of consistency doesn't matter as much and wouldn't really even be possible because students select their own courses in second and third year based on their personal interests, their preferred professors, and even their preferred methods of evaluation. (They also may just want to avoid taking classes on Fridays and Mondays.)

TN: *After studying philosophy at university for four years, investigating evaluation patterns at Canadian law schools was very enlightening. These forms of evaluation – particularly the continuing importance still placed on final exams – seem quite different from my undergrad experience. Almost every course I took while earning my undergraduate degree had a midterm and a final as well as writing assignments that were due throughout the year. By the time the final exam rolled around, you already had a good idea of what your final mark in the course was likely going to be. It seems that is just not always or even usually the case for law school courses. Law students might leave their final exam not having a clue about whether they are likely to receive an A or an F in the course, or anything in between.*

CN: Happily, F grades at Canadian law schools are very rare. Canadian law schools have, for many years, operated on the more humane basis that was once offered as a justification for using the LSAT to improve law school admissions processes: It is very difficult to gain admission into law school in the first place, so very few students who are admitted are likely to lack the academic ability to succeed once there. A (or "High Honours") grades are also usually "rationed" in one way or another as well, for reasons we will discuss later in this chapter. So, most law students in large courses evaluated with a final exam receive course grades that fall between these two extremes, typically in the B– to B+ range (or, if the law school is using a "Pass with Merit"/"Low Pass"/"Honours"/"High Honours" system, most often a grade of either "Pass with Merit" or "Honours.")

Summative and Formative Assessments

TN: I know that there is a well-known distinction between "summative" and "formative" assessments. A final exam seems to be the classic example of "summative" assessment. It comes at the end of the course. It is designed to evaluate how well a student has learned the material but, frankly, the evaluation is too late for the student to learn from their exam performance or to take any steps to modify their approach to learning the material, other than perhaps in the most general way in respect of how to approach future courses. But those future courses would be in different subjects and likely taught by different professors.

It seems as though law schools rely on summative assessment more heavily than many other undergraduate university programs do. I wonder why law schools don't make greater use of formative assessment: the sort of interim, regular evaluation that occurs while the course is still ongoing? Formative assessments can help the student and the professor gauge the student's progress and perhaps make adjustments or improvements before it's too late.

CN: Evaluation methods and grading policies and procedures are, not surprisingly, a regular subject of discussion and debate among law school professors and law students.

Although law schools are sometimes criticized for relying more heavily on final exams than on more frequent formative assessments, final exams may actually be more helpful to student learning than we sometimes give them credit for because of a well-known phenomenon known as the testing effect.[2] But final exams are not the final word. Students will certainly see examples of formative assessment used in law school as well. Midterm quizzes and short assignments like critical reflection papers are common law school examples of formative assessment. Midterm tests help provide feedback early enough in the academic term that a course correction is still possible. Writing assignments of various kinds can also help students practise their legal research skills and improve their legal writing and analytical skills.

2 "Many experimental studies, however, indicate that taking tests also facilitates students' learning. Often, the accessibility of previously retrieved learning material is enhanced in a later, final test – a phenomenon called the testing effect ... In this context, the focus of testing is shifted from the assessment of learning outcomes to supporting the learning process – assessment for learning rather than assessment of learning." Juliane Schwieren, Jonathan Barenberg and Stephan Dutke, "The Testing Effect in the Psychology Classroom: A Meta-Analytic Perspective" (2017) 16:2 *Psychology Learning and Teaching* 179 at 180.

TN: It goes without saying that formative assessment is only valuable if the professor's response is timely. I've heard some law students complain that some assignments aren't actually returned until the course is over. A midterm quiz that isn't graded and returned to the student until the course is over is really just a mid-course summative assessment. It does nothing to help the student improve or refine their approach to learning the course material. It comes too late, like a medical diagnosis that is made after the patient has died.

CN: Written tests and assignments are not the only forms of effective formative assessment. In a law school class where the professor uses the Socratic method, student participation in Socratic questioning and answering can also be seen as one very effective (though not always popular) type of formative assessment. Formative assessment doesn't necessarily involve graded assignments. But assigning marks for student participation can encourage students to attend class regularly, keep up with the reading material, and regularly practise recalling and analyzing that material. Speaking in class in response to a professor's questions might also be good practice for someone who wants to argue in court some day.

Final Exams

So what about the continuing use in law schools of final exams in many courses? Well, although I am not a fan of final exams – especially 100 percent final exams – I must admit one thing about them: They can provide motivation. This is a simple insight that I received from a current law student:

> Remember that the final exam is always coming. It will be examining you on everything you have learned the whole year. So don't forget to always have the exam in the back of your mind: every class you attend, every case you read, every note you take. In everything you do, remember, you are preparing yourself for the final exam.

As a motivator, in other words, a final exam can be pretty powerful. Samuel Johnson said, "When a man knows he is to be hanged in a fortnight, it concentrates his mind wonderfully."[3] It seems when law students know they are to be examined in a couple of months, that also helps concentrate their minds. That, presumably, is one reason that some law professors still use them in spite of all the valid criticisms of 100 percent final exams that have been made over the years.

Do Exams Really Help You Learn the Material, or Do They Just Help You Learn How to Cram?

It seems like obvious advice, but when an exam is a whole term or even a whole school year away, it can be easy to forget what you are working toward. Also, who do you think is likely going to do better on the 100 percent final? The student who diligently attends class all year, taking careful notes, regularly reviewing the materials they have been assigned throughout the term to ensure they have a full and detailed understanding of the course? Or the student who skips every class until the very last month of the term, relies on borrowed notes from other

3 James Boswell, *Boswell's Life of Johnson* (New York: Henry Frowde, 1904) at 127.

students (who may or may not have been any more diligent), crams for a day or two before the exam, and then finds to their shock and horror that there is a major question on the exam based on material that was assigned back in the first week of class in September? I mean, which student do you want to be?

Now, to be fair, law students have told me I'm dead wrong about this. They say their experience in law school doesn't necessarily support the idea that regular hard work over the course of a term pays off. You can be the hardest working student in class, they tell me, do all the readings assigned (even do extra readings), be part of a study group, and sacrifice your entire social life, and it doesn't matter. You can still end up getting a lower grade than some slacker who just happens to be a brilliant exam writer, the sort of person who can skim someone else's course summary (also called outlines or CANs, short for Condensed Annotated Notes), then just waltz into the exam with a few prewritten generic answers, yet still somehow manages to be on the same wavelength as the professor. It can be very discouraging, they tell me.

Hard work, they say, just doesn't always seem to pay off in law school. Grading seems to be almost random. Work day and night for the whole term, and you'll get a B. Wait until the last minute and cram, you'll still get a B. Remember the old joke about professors marking exams by throwing them down the stairs – the exams that land on the higher steps get higher grades, the exams that land on the lower steps get the lower grades? Well, that really seems to be an accurate picture of what happens at law school, according to some law students, except that most of the exams seem to be mysteriously touching down on the "B" step.

I have to take these people at their word. They have been to law school . . . I haven't. On the other hand, I don't know how easy it is to accurately compare your own effort in a course, let alone your performance on an exam, with all the other students in the class. If most people in a class are actually working very hard (including those people who are working very hard behind the scenes but who have mastered the art of pretending they can succeed effortlessly), maybe it isn't surprising that it is so difficult to stand out from the law school crowd on the basis of hard work alone. In other words, maybe the hard work and the other sacrifices that law students make may not have been wasted after all. Maybe the more important question to ask is, how much lower might your mark have been if you hadn't been so diligent and made all those sacrifices?

But that's a question that I won't be able to answer here. What I will try to do instead is to explore some aspects of law school evaluation and see whether these offer any clues about how to get the most out of law school courses.

Closed-Book vs Open-Book Exams

Everyone agrees that you can expect to find that most final law school exams are open book. Students can bring in their textbooks, their notes, and usually most other printed materials as well. Many professors prefer to use open-book exams because, well, life is open book. Most lawyers aren't expected to answer complex legal questions off the top of their head from memory. But a few professors at some schools apparently disagree. They prefer to use closed-book exams, sometimes with some modifications. For example, they might provide students on the day of the exam with a copy of the table of contents for the course case book, or with a list of the names of all of the cases referred to in the course. Or they might let students bring in a single sheet of paper filled with as many notes as they can manage to fit on it, and so on.

I personally have always preferred a closed-book exam, for two reasons. One, the questions on a closed-book exam tend to be less specific since the professor who wrote the exam knows you don't have access to the textbook or your notes. And two, I believe I can study better for a closed-book exam precisely because I know I won't be able to rely on bringing in any material. The way I study for a closed-book exam gives me an overall better understanding of the material because I really have to learn it – not simply memorize it, but really understand it, deeply, for the exam.

That, again, has only been my personal experience based on closed-book exams in university. Law school exams might well be different. I'm not, nor have I ever been, a law student. I, like you, am still trying to decide if law school is right for me. And I'm trying to do that based on more information than just watching and rewatching *Legally Blonde*. (Incredible film, by the way. I would highly recommend it. Spoiler alert: It's not a documentary.)

Whether an open-book exam seems easier for you or harder will likely depend on individual characteristics like your memory, powers of organization, and the specific way you happen to respond to stress. But your overall grade in a law school course might not be affected very much regardless of whether an exam is open or closed book for the reason discussed in the next section: law school courses are usually marked on a "class average."

Class Averages

You have probably heard the old joke about the two campers who find themselves about to be chased by a hungry bear. One camper leans down for an instant to make sure the laces on his running shoes are tied. "What are you doing?" the second camper says. "You can't outrun a bear!" "I know," the first camper answers. "But I don't need to outrun the bear. I just need to outrun you."

This tasteless joke is surprisingly relevant to law school evaluation. Most Canadian law schools grade on the basis of some sort of class average or a mandatory grade distribution (that is, like the famous Gaussian or "bell" curve).

Because most law schools grade on the basis of some sort of class average, a law student's grade in any particular class depends entirely on whether that student outperforms or underperforms the other students in the class. This is something that is important to keep in mind about law school grades, and I'm told law students learn this very early on.

There are a lot fewer students in a first-year law class than a typical first-year university undergraduate class, where students may number in the hundreds. And if only 10–15 percent of students are allowed to get As, then you're going to have to do a lot more work to earn that A than simply showing up at your professor's office after the exam and begging them to raise your mark. (Not implying you would ever do that. My only point is, it isn't likely to work at law school where grades are treated a little more like controlled substances than they are in many undergraduate courses.)

So it's going to be harder in law school to score the high marks many students get used to in undergrad. And that can be tough on the ego, especially for people who have been "A" students all their lives. Suddenly you may find that, at least among all the other super-achieving "A" students, you are pretty much average. Among the "As," in other words, you're a "B."

The method of grading on a class average or institutionally mandated grading distribution is referred to as "norm-based" grading. Norm-based grading is an alternative to "standards-based" or "criteria-based" grading, where every student who achieves some clearly specified course standards can achieve the same (high) grade.

Is this really the best, fairest, and most reliable method of grading?

TN: Some law students argue that marking on a class average in a way that is common at most law schools is unfair. Why can't students get the marks they have earned and deserve? If everyone has earned an A on an exam, why should professors be forced to exaggerate the small differences in students' performances to come up with a distribution of grades that meets some arbitrary grading "curve" or satisfies an artificially low "B" class average?

CN: One curious thing one might note about that argument is that if the same sort of approach had applied to everyone's undergraduate university experience, arguably, dare we say that perhaps a few of the law students who are now objecting might not have been admitted to law school in the first place. What I mean is, some of the very same people who have benefited throughout their high school and university careers from receiving higher grades and test scores than their classmates now would prefer if grades could be a little more evened out. Big grade distinctions may have helped them get into law school, but they would like law schools to reduce such big distinctions now that they are no longer the people receiving the highest grades.

TN: But maybe these students are right and maybe the other faculties are also right to use standards-based grading. Why do so many law schools use class average grading?

CN: The main argument in favour of class average grading is that it helps preserve grading consistency between classes and professors, and law schools have tried a little harder than many other university undergraduate programs to hold the line on grade inflation. Standard class averages also prevent people from "shopping" for easier professors and easier courses instead of choosing those courses that would be of the most interest or most long-term value for the students.

There may also be something about the nature of the knowledge and skills that are involved in law school courses that differs from the sort of course material that can be wholly mastered by every diligent student and so evaluated on the basis of straightforward criteria that everyone can satisfy. Studying law is not like learning how to perform a mechanical task that can be broken down into steps and then thoroughly mastered, like learning to drive a car with a stick shift. "Mastery learning" applies when every student in a class can fully and completely understand the material – all at the same level of understanding or "mastery" – before moving on.[4] Law school does not seem to be quite like that.

4 See, e.g., Imed Bouchrika, "What Is Mastery Learning Model? Definitsion, Principles, and Examples for 2025," Research.com (April 7, 2025), online: https://research.com/education/what-is-mastery-learning.

Studying law is more like studying the works of Aristotle. Everyone can be assigned the readings and can have interesting and valuable individual perspectives to offer in class discussions. But not everyone will come to understand things with quite the same degree of depth, nuance, insight, and originality. And it would be impossible to expect that the class would wait to move on until everyone had reached some readily defined "mastery" level of interpretation and understanding of the work.

TN: *In other words, you're saying that law seems to be more like studying Aristotle than learning to drive a car with a stick shift. Maybe that should have been the subtitle of this book?*

I'm still not entirely convinced by the argument for the "norm-based," class average grading of law schools. Many people have criticized this approach to law school grading. Couldn't law schools consider adopting some kind of standards-based grading? Is there really a compelling justification for the existing system? Is it really important, for example, to limit the number of As that can be awarded in any given course? It must be the case that in some classes students all did exceptionally well – much better, on average, than in past years or in other classes, for example. Why can't every student who has done excellent work get an A?

CN: There are not many examples of exceptional endeavours in the world that don't involve some kind of "rationing" of honours. Perhaps the benefit of this rationing is that it provides an incentive for everyone to achieve their personal best. Some readers may remember watching the 100-metre final in the 2024 Olympics. There were eight runners in that race. The gold medal went to Noah Lyles of the United States. His time was 9.784 seconds. The silver medal went to Kishane Thompson of Jamaica, whose time was 9.789 seconds. The "slowest" runner in that final was Oblique Seville, also from Jamaica. Of course, Seville wasn't slow at all. He finished eighth, but he ran the race in a lightning-paced 9.91 seconds – in other words, just .13 of a second slower than Noah Lyles. Less than half a second was the difference between the glory of the gold medal and the obscurity of finishing last in the final.

Why didn't the Olympic officials simply say, "Well, we had an unusually strong group of runners this year. It's unfair to draw huge distinctions between them when they were all so close, so we are going to award them all a gold medal"? Because encouraging and rewarding achievement at the very highest level doesn't work that way.

Of course, we recognize that overall performance in a given course, or a given exam, or even an entire law school cohort may be exceptionally strong in any given year. In fact, in athletics we fully expect the overall standard of performance does, objectively, improve year over year. The world record holders of a generation ago would barely qualify to participate in many Olympic sporting events today. The same rising general level of standards could well be true of law students as well. The overall quality of Canadian law schools today might be far higher than it was 50 years ago. But our grades do not, and cannot, speak to how law students today compare to the law students of half a century ago. Our grades are only intended to measure, to the best of the evaluator's (all-too-human, admittedly imperfect) ability, the relative performance of a student within a particular class.

This important message – that law school grades in each course are relative – is sometimes obscured by the fact that universities also frequently publish statements in their academic calendars or websites purporting to explain what their institution's grades supposedly "mean" in absolute terms. These statements should make clear that they do not necessarily apply to the grades awarded in any faculty that uses "class average" grading. After all, if the narrative grade explanations really meant what they said, there would be no mandatory class averages imposed by academic units, including law schools. Class average grading in such a case would be both unnecessary and incoherent.

We might expect, especially in a large class, that the performance of students would roughly fall into the familiar Gaussian (or "bell curve") distribution pattern: most grades would cluster around an average (or median) and one would see a relatively smaller number of grades that deviated from the average grade – either higher or lower. In that case, a faculty-mandated "B" average, for example, would simply serve to require professors to designate as "B" whatever was found to be the average performance of students in class.

Perhaps, based on the professor's initial marking scheme, for example, most students achieved 90 percent on their exam – with a few receiving marks in the 80s, and a few receiving 95–100 percent. Since 90 percent was the average grade achieved by students in the class, in a class with a mandatory "B" average, every student achieving 90 percent on that initial marking scheme would be awarded a grade of "B." The same reasoning would, incidentally, apply on an exam where most students achieved, on an initial grading scheme, a mark of just 40 percent – with a few receiving marks in the 30s and a handful receiving marks between 50–60 percent. On such an exam, a student achieving 40 percent on the initial marking scheme would be awarded a "B."

In each case, the "B" grade means the same thing: This student's performance, relative to the other students in this particular class, was about average. One professor may have set an exam that was, frankly, unusually easy. Another may have set an exam that was unusually challenging. That is the reason the initial "marks" have no absolute meaning. Their only purpose is to provide a way to rank students on a fair and principled basis. Their final grades will reflect that ranking – nothing more, except in the rare case of failing grades, when an objective judgment is made that the student's work has not satisfied the necessary requirements.

After all, when one talks about grades in a professional school, surely we must assume that everyone who passes has achieved a sufficient level of competence that they can eventually satisfy the demanding standards of their chosen profession. And everyone understands that admission to law school is highly competitive. So it may be presumed that every law student is likely to be well above average in terms of academic ability[5] when compared with the

5 Behavioral psychologists, incidentally, tell us that research shows the average person believes themself to be of above average intelligence. See, e.g., Orville G Brim, Jr, "College Grades and Self-Estimates of Intelligence" (1954) 45:8 J Educ Psych 477; and Patrick R Heck et al, "65% of Americans Believe They Are Above Average in Intelligence" (2018) 13:7 PLoS One, online: https://pmc.ncbi.nlm.nih.gov/articles/PMC6029792/pdf/pone.0200103.pdf. This phenomenon is sometimes facetiously referred to as the "Lake Wobegon Effect," an allusion to the

university student population generally. In other words, we expect every professional school graduate to have achieved sufficient mastery of the essential subject matter. That is really what an average passing grade in a professional school should mean.

In short, it is earning the JD degree itself that is the primary goal and that signals a major accomplishment. Graduating with a JD degree signifies having achieved the necessary (and very high) standard of competence demanded by all of Canada's highly selective law schools. Grades, then, are only necessary for the secondary purpose of ranking relative performance within this very accomplished and privileged group of students. If everyone could be awarded an A grade in every course, assigning grades at law school would be an entirely pointless exercise.

TN: That pointlessness might be, well, the point.

How Can Students Perform Well on Law School Exams?

TN: We've talked in a general way about law school evaluation and in particular about law school exams. But what we haven't talked about is what those exams might actually look like and what students might need to know to do their best on them.

CN: There are many different types of law school exam questions – including, from time to time, multiple-choice, short answer, and theory or policy-based essay questions. But the

fictional town of Lake Wobegon featured in the written and radio works of author Garrison Keillor. See Garrison Keillor, *Lake Wobegon Days* (New York: Penguin Books, 1985).

one sort of question that is unique to law school exams is the hypothetical fact problem.

A hypothetical law school exam problem will describe a complex series of usually quite improbable facts that raise legal issues that have been discussed in the readings and in the classes throughout the terms. Sometimes those facts will seem very familiar because they will mirror the circumstances described in specific decided cases that were studied in class. At other times, however, the professor will combine elements of different cases, weaving and entangling legal issues in a way that challenges students not only to recognize and apply specific legal principles to situations that are similar to those studied in the course, but also to go beyond the parameters of the case book and consider how to analyze the legal implications of fact scenarios that raise complex intersecting issues, each of which lies at the very outer edge of the very greyest areas of the law.

A torts exam, for example, may well include a hypothetical fact problem describing a tragic series of unfortunate and highly improbable accidents, each one of which may (or may not) involve tortious actions or omissions on the part of the fictitious hypothetical characters. The question may then ask students to assume they have been retained by a specific character in the scenario and to advise that character as to any legal actions they might be able to pursue or that might be brought against them. Or perhaps the question might simply ask, more generally, "Based on these facts, who can sue whom and for what?"

In every case, the objective of the question is to test the student's knowledge of the relevant legal principles and their ability to analyze those principles intelligently, coherently, and creatively in the particular context of a complex pattern of facts, drawing on relevant authority, including common law cases and, where applicable, statutes. And, of course, since language is so critical to legal exposition, analysis, and advocacy, exams also test students' ability to write in a clear, concise, persuasive, and engaging way.

Where students most often go astray in responding to such hypothetical problems is by failing to engage with the specific facts as presented in the problem. Too often, some students appear to believe that the best exam-writing strategy involves coming into the examination room clutching a set of lengthy, generic "prewrites" (or, more likely, with a number of such prewrites saved as readily accessible files on their laptops). Expecting, for example, that their torts exam is likely to include a question about negligence, they prepare in advance a general recitation of all the basic features of negligence law, complete with case citations for each of the constituent elements. Finding a hypothetical fact problem that does, indeed, seem to touch on the law of negligence, they triumphantly transcribe their "prewrite" verbatim. The prewritten answer may well refer to many aspects of the law of negligence that actually have no relevance whatsoever to the specific facts contained in the exam problem. But why should that matter, they reason? After all, every detail of the prewrite is correct. And isn't reciting the law correctly what the professor will be looking for?

Unfortunately, on a law school exam (and in a lawyer's office and a courtroom too, for that matter), recognizing which issues are *not* raised by a given set of facts can be just as important as identifying the issues that *are* raised. Though some brief, succinct, *relevant* general statement of the law may well serve as a helpful prologue for an effective examination answer, it is essential for students to move beyond a vague statement of general principles that merely hover above the facts of the exam problem. Knowledge of the law is, of course, expected. But you must apply the law to the facts. Be as specific as possible. Take a position and advocate for that position, acknowledging fairly, and refuting effectively, reasonable counterarguments.

And, just as good trial judges must frequently do, remember to argue in the alternative. You may be convinced that no successful argument could possibly be raised to establish the liability of a hypothetical defendant; so you conclude there is no reason to waste any time discussing the principles that might apply to an assessment of damages if that defendant were to be found liable. Alas, your professor may have a marking rubric for the question that includes a number of marks to be awarded for an astute analysis of your hypothetical defendant's damages. So admit fallibility. There is no weakness in that. The decisions of Superior Court judges are often overturned by the Court of Appeal. For that matter, there are frequently dissenting judgments in Supreme Court of Canada cases that are harshly critical of the majority judgment. So, argue in the alternative, just to be on the safe side: "If my conclusion is wrong, and the defendant is found liable, the plaintiff's damages will be determined in the following way . . ."

Nor should you overlook the role the exam question has asked you to play. Are you expected to advocate on behalf of the plaintiff? Then make the plaintiff's case. And make it a persuasive case, too. The law school exam is no place for dry recitation of information. Argue as persuasively as you can. That doesn't mean ignoring valid points that might be made for the other side. Quite the contrary. A persuasive argument is not one that ignores plausible counterarguments but is one that meets the best argument of one's opponent head on – presents it fairly, as strongly as anyone could make it, then tears it down again, brick by brick.

In short, the exam is no place for timid, general statements. It is a chance for you to shine, to show what you have learned to the one person in all the world who is most interested – the professor who has taught the course and drafted the exam. Try to see the challenge presented by the exam as the professor has undoubtedly seen it: not as some wretched trial aimed at revealing what students do not know, but as a golden opportunity to proudly show what you have learned and how well you can apply that knowledge as you use your own unique perspective to analyze, reason, and persuade.

Anonymous Grading

TN: *Let's speak a little more specifically about grading practices. I understand that, to try to increase objectivity and impartiality, law school grading is done on an anonymous basis. How does that work?*

CN: Law school examinations at Canadian law schools are almost invariably graded on an anonymous basis. Students are assigned an anonymous identification number or pseudonym by the law school administrative office and that number – and only that number – appears on the examination that is seen and graded by the professor. Anonymous grading eliminates concerns of both favouritism and unfair prejudice. Professors may not always be entirely consistent in their grading, but one may rest assured that no grading decision has been made based on any personal considerations.

Grades on essays and other written assignments that involve prior approval of topics or consultation before final submission may be different. They cannot always be evaluated anonymously and so, in the view of some, may not be as reliably objective as examination grades. There may always be a concern that, as a matter of human nature, professors who get to know students in a small class might feel disinclined to give some students lower grades even when, perhaps, that is what their work might merit. Such a result may be very much welcomed by some students in that professor's class. But the impact of grading reaches beyond the walls of each individual classroom. When future employers or perhaps graduate school admissions officers review and compare students' transcripts, the effect of overly generous grading in one course is to indirectly and unfairly punish students who have taken other more judicially graded courses instead.

Now, some law professors strongly resist the argument that a relative grading scheme makes grades more useful for prospective employers. Why should law schools, they argue, be in the business of making it easier for wealthy, powerful law firms to recruit new lawyers? Universities are in the business of educating students, not providing free advance screening of job applicants. Evaluating potential job candidates, frankly, is the employers' problem, isn't it?

This is a compelling argument in principle. But it may have to yield to harsh practical considerations. If there was only one law school in Canada from which all Canadian law firms, governments, businesses, and other employers hired articling students or new lawyers, the argument that law schools should be indifferent to the preferences of prospective employers might well prevail. But because law firms and other employers tend to recruit students from across the country, a law school would be doing its students a grave disservice if it made it unduly difficult or even practically impossible for prospective employers to identify those students attending any one of several different schools that are most likely to be able to manage the demands of complex areas of practice. While the educational mission of Canadian law schools is nuanced, as a practical matter we know that most students begin their law school careers (and make necessary sacrifices to pay their tuition to do so) with the hope that their law degree will one day help them pursue a career in law. The road to such a career often runs through the offices of large national law firms, and comparable grades are, for better or worse, the toll that hopeful lawyers must pay to travel that road. Law schools cannot realistically ignore this very reasonable student expectation.

Law School, Not Lawyer School (Sounds Familiar)

Yet again, then, it seems we come back to a familiar point from previous chapters: Law school isn't necessarily (just) lawyer school. Exams are not just designed to see if you would make a good lawyer or if you can argue effectively in court. They are also designed to motivate you to spend time thinking deeply about the areas of law you are studying – both in and out of class – and to test your ability to analyze, to reason (in the special legal way), and to write clearly and persuasively. So even though it looks really fun to close deals and cross-examine witnesses like Harvey Specter (yes, he gets to do both), you need to master a lot of specific law school skills before you ever get the chance to try your hand at the more practical aspects of being a lawyer. And no, unlike Mike Ross,[6] you can't actually beat the system and simply bypass law school!

6 Fun fact. *Suits* was filmed in Toronto, and I had the pleasure of meeting Patrick J Adams, the actor who plays Mike Ross, when they were shooting a scene at the University of Toronto. He asked me if I was a lawyer. It turns out that, even in real life, it is hard to tell one way or another just by looking at someone. It was awesome.

9

moot courts and mock trials

Introduction

It was one of my favourite episodes of *Suits*: the mock trial, pitting genius pretend-lawyer Mike Ross, representing himself as the accused, against his savvy mentor, Harvey Specter, playing the prosecutor. The mock trial in *Suits* was staged in the offices of a law firm, not at a law school. But it is usually at law school where students practise their advocacy skills by participating in mock trials and moot courts. We want to explore them a little more closely in this chapter.

Moot courts have been around for a very long time. In fact, moot courts had been part of lawyers' education in England years before there were any law schools. Moots were part of barristers' training at the English Inns of Court as early as the fourteenth century. One author has even gone so far as to say that moot courts weren't just *part* of a lawyer's education in those days, moots "literally were the legal education of those who sought to become lawyers."[1]

In North America, moots for students started around the same time that university law schools began to be established. They have been part of the Harvard Law School student experience since the 1830s.[2]

So what is mooting, and how does it work at Canadian law schools?

What Is a Moot?

TN: What, exactly, is a moot (or a moot court)?

CN: Let's start with the word "moot." Historically, the word "moot" derives from an Old English word that meant "meet" or "assembly," and it may have had some link to a physical place where people assembled to discuss and deal with important community issues. When people outside of law school use the word "moot" today as an adjective, they are usually dismissing something as "irrelevant," "of no practical importance," or "of academic interest only." Suppose someone were to ask, "What colour uniforms would the Toronto Maple Leafs wear when playing home games in the Stanley Cup Final?" Someone might answer, "Well that's a moot point. The Leafs aren't going to be in the Stanley Cup Final."

1 Andrew Lynch, "Why Do We Moot? Exploring the Role of Mooting in Legal Education" (1996) 7:1 Legal Educ Rev 67.
2 Darby Dickerson, "In Re Moot Court" (2000) 29:4 Stetson L Rev 1217 at 1223.

TN: Or will they?[3]

CN: The word "moot" can also be used as a verb. The verb "moot" means to raise or propose something for debate or discussion. For example, "the idea of introducing more practical training for students in law school has often been mooted."

In the corridors of law schools, the word "moot" is used a little differently. The word "moot" is used by law students either as an adjective modifying "court" or on its own as a noun (technically, a nominalized adjective) meaning exactly the same thing: a moot court. It also seems to be used by law students as a verb referring to the act of participating in a moot. For example, "I was in a moot last term. I discovered I really enjoy mooting."

A "moot" or a "moot court," then, is a simulated litigation exercise. But the phrase "moot court" and the word "moot" on its own are often used by law students in a more specific way to refer to one particular kind of simulated litigation exercise: a simulated hearing before an appeal court, like the Supreme Court of Canada or one of the provincial courts of appeal, or perhaps a hearing involving a fictional dispute between two countries before an international tribunal such as the International Court of Justice. What these sorts of moots have in common is that law students who participate in them make oral arguments that only involve disputes over issues of law and that are only made in front of a panel of judges, not a jury. They don't have to prove any

---

3 It should be mentioned that at the time of writing the Leafs had just made it through the first round of the 2025 NHL playoffs, so ... [Authors' note: During the final editing stages of this book, the Leafs were knocked out of the playoffs by the Florida Panthers, who went on to win the Stanley Cup. So it was a moot point after all.]

facts. They are given the facts by the organizers of the moot in the form of a hypothetical problem or perhaps a real or fictitious tribunal or court decision. That means they don't have to present any evidence. There are no witnesses, no examinations in chief, no cross-examination, and no one standing up yelling "I object!" In short, there is none of the drama that makes trials (and even mock trials) exciting.

Law students do participate in other sorts of practice exercises, too, including mock trials. But mock trials aren't nearly as common as moots because they involve much more elaborate preparation and organization and require the involvement of many people other than the law students who are playing the lawyers and the professors or perhaps upper-year students who are acting as judges. People are needed to act the parts of all the witnesses, for instance, and these actors may each have to prepare significantly in advance to play their roles effectively, otherwise the whole mock trial will be an utter waste of time. You may need to recruit people to serve as jurors as well. It's all pretty time and resource intensive, and it can be a real scheduling challenge.

Moots are much more manageable. Mooting at law school isn't just done as a classroom learning exercise. It can also be a competitive activity. Law students from different law schools compete against one another in various moot court competitions. We've included in Appendix D at the end of this chapter a list of some of the mooting and similar competitions that many Canadian law schools participate in.

Some of these competitive "moots" involve different kinds of practice simulation exercises. For example, in addition to simulated appeal court or international tribunal arguments, a competitive moot may involve a simulated hearing before an administrative tribunal, a mock arbitration, a mock negotiation, or even perhaps a full-blown mock trial like the Mike Ross/Harvey Specter showdown mentioned earlier.

Some Moot Points

TN: I know that moots have been taking place at law schools for years, even centuries. But how do they fit within the law school curriculum? Are there moot court courses? Are they included as part of other courses? Are they extracurricular or co-curricular activities?

CN: Yes.

TN: Yes?

CN: I mean that they can be all of those things. At most law schools, law students are required to participate in a moot in their first year, usually as part of a legal research and writing program. Students might first be given a hypothetical fact problem – a more elaborate version of the sort of problem that often appears on law school exams, as we discussed in chapter 8 – and be asked to prepare a research memo on the legal issues raised by the problem. Then, they might later use that research memo as the basis for drafting a "factum."

TN: What is a factum?

CN: A factum is a written argument prepared when a decision by a lower court is being appealed. It includes a brief outline of the facts, a recitation of the specific legal issues that the court is being asked to decide, the arguments legal counsel is making to support its side of the case, and a clear statement of the order or relief or remedy the party submitting the factum is seeking from the court.

The basic requirements for factums[4] are found in provincial rules of civil procedure. For example, in Ontario, the basic requirements are found in Rule 4.06.1 of the Ontario *Rules of Civil Procedure.*[5] Incidentally, although written arguments are used in court processes around the world, the word "factum" to refer to such arguments appears to be unique to Canada.[6] (The comparable document in the United States, for example, is called a brief.)

When a moot takes the form of a simulated argument before the International Court of Justice – as it does, for example, in the case of the Philip C Jessup International Law Moot Court Competition, the world's largest competitive law school moot – the terminology is different. There, the written statement of facts and legal arguments prepared by each party is referred to as a "memorial," the term used in the International Court of Justice's *Rules of Court.*[7]

---

4 Sometimes people prefer to use the word "facta" as the plural of "factum," because they assume that "factum" is a second declension neuter Latin noun that forms its plural that way. But the origin of the word as a legal term is complicated. It may have come into English through a French word for "pamphlet" or "brochure." For a wonderful discussion of this history, see the article referred to in note 6, below. In any event, whatever the true etymology, the *Rules of Civil Procedure* uses the word "factums" not "facta" as the plural. So that is the convention we will follow here.

5 RRO 1990, Reg 194.

6 See Jean E Coté, "History of Factums" (2014) 52:1 Alta L Rev 71. (The author of this fascinating history of the factum is the Honourable Jean Coté, a former judge of the Alberta Court of Appeal.)

7 Online: https://www.icj-cij.org/rules.

TN: Once students have drafted their factums, what happens next?

CN: The next step is the moot itself. The moot typically takes the form of the oral argument in an appeal from a lower court decision. The professor plays the role of the appeal court judge, and the students play the role either of counsel for the appellant (the party that is trying to overturn the lower court decision) or counsel for the respondent (the party that originally won the case and hopes to have that lower court decision upheld.)

Each party is given a specific amount of time to present their oral arguments. It is usually a fairly limited amount of time. But what really distinguishes a moot from a debate or a public speaking contest is that the judge will interrupt the student with questions – seeking clarification, testing the limits of the position the student is taking, and so on.

TN: It sounds like a fairly gruelling experience.

CN: It can certainly be an intense experience. But it can also be pretty exhilarating. Remember that the judge – typically your professor in the case of a first-year, compulsory moot – isn't trying to embarrass you. They are trying to give you a chance to engage with the material in a livelier and more spontaneous way and, perhaps, to challenge you to think about the issues raised by the moot problem in ways that hadn't necessarily occurred to you. Although many students find the *idea* of moots stressful and a bit intimidating, after they have actually done their first-year moot, most students report that they are not only relieved but that they genuinely enjoyed the experience. Moots are fun. They are exciting. They are an intense and invaluable learning experience.

In addition to the compulsory moot, which is usually a part of the first-year curriculum, many law schools also organize an optional competitive moot for first-year students. There may also be some limited opportunities for first-year students to enter competitive mooting competitions with law students from other law schools.

After first year, there are more ways for students who are interested in mooting to gain additional mooting experience. Some professors in upper-year courses might offer students the chance to do a moot as an optional grading exercise. Some law schools organize an upper-year intramural moot court competition as an optional co-curricular exercise.

These intramural upper-year moots at some schools serve as a gateway to participating in one of the many competitive moots to which most Canadian law schools send representative teams.

Years ago, participating in an upper-year competitive moot was an extracurricular activity for law students, like representing your school on a sports team. But today it is much more common for law schools to offer course credit to students who are competing in these moots. Being selected to represent your law school on one of these competitive mooting teams is regarded by many students as highly desirable not only because the mooting experience itself is intrinsically rewarding but also because they have the chance to earn course credits taking a course that is not typically subject to the usual "B" or "B+" class average that we discussed in chapter 8.

Over time, as law schools have broadened the type of experiential learning available to students to include things like simulated arbitrations, negotiations, and client counselling, as well as mock trials and moot courts, competitions involving these other sorts of skills have also proliferated, and often some of these competitions are also broadly referred to as moots as well.

The Case for and against Moots

There is a wide range of opinions among law professors about the value and utility of moots. I am for the most part very much in favour of them. Moots offer a great experience for students. These are certainly exercises in advocacy, but not in oral advocacy alone. Most moot court competitions require participants to draft factums, the formal written arguments provided to the court in advance of the oral hearing. The exercise is, therefore, one of legal research and writing as well as oral argument.

Preparing for a moot and presenting and defending your arguments orally is a challenging and rewarding experience. In some ways, well-argued moots before a well-prepared and lively bench represent a return to the most rigorous form of the Socratic method, which can help students develop confidence and poise along with a much better practical understanding of how to translate abstract legal ideas into clear and convincing arguments.

Moots also give students a chance to work collaboratively with their fellow team members in the analysis of a legal problem – a skill that is in some ways a more accurate reflection of practice experience than the solitary library work that is typical of many other law school research exercises.

Finally, it has also been argued that coaching moot court teams can be a valuable pedagogical experience from the perspective of the professor/coach.[8] And of course, some people have called moots a law school "rite of passage." Now, a "rite of passage" isn't necessarily a valuable or essential educational experience. At the University of Oxford, for example, it is traditional for students to wear carnations when they write their examinations. They're colour coded depending on whether a student is writing their first exam (white), their last exam (red), or one of the exams in between (pink). Following this simple custom might well be seen as a time-honoured rite of passage, too. It's a very old tradition, and it makes things very colourful on the streets of Oxford around exam time. But no one would argue that wearing a carnation is essential to a person's education.

And frankly, as valuable as moots can be, I do have some reservations about the demands moots can often place on students' already scarce time. I am especially worried that some students – especially first-year law students – could be unduly distracted by mooting from the other fundamental aspects of the first-year law experience, each of which has its own set of rewards and can represent a once-in-a-lifetime educational opportunity.

Some people have raised much more sweeping objections to mooting at law school. First, some critics complain that the "skills" emphasized in mooting competitions are superficial presentation skills. They complain that many of the "tips"

---

8 David W Case, "A Pedagogical Rationale for the Law Professor as Moot Court Coach" (2020) 89:3 Miss LJ 367.

given to mooters by judges have little or nothing to do with helping them improve their proficiency in research, reasoning, analysis, or their legal knowledge generally. Instead, mooters may be told to "smile more," "look the judges in the eye," "don't speak in a monotone," "slow down," "speed up," "don't fidget," "use hand gestures a little more," "keep your hands still," "try not to look at your notes so much," and "don't say 'um'."

One particularly harsh critic of moots has summarized his contempt for the supposedly dubious value of law school moots in this way: "Jessup is just another law student moot court competition in which style trumps substance, and where good used car salesmen typically come out on top."[9] Another critic has condemned moots as not only wrongly focused on presentation style rather than genuine persuasiveness, but also as wholly unrealistic and of no academic or vocational benefit to students, not even as a résumé builder. As he rather harshly puts it, "The simple fact is that when it comes to getting a job, moot court has squat resumé value."[10]

Of course, moots have their vigorous defenders, too.[11] And it should go without saying that the fact that the number of competitive moots and the number of students participating in competitive moots continues to grow rather than shrink at

---

9 Dan Joyner, "Why I Won't Attend the Jessup Competition Again," *Opinio Juris* (13 February 2012), quoted in David M Scott & Ukri Soirila, "The Politics of the Moot Court" (2021) 32:3 Eur J Int'l L 1079 at 1081.

10 Alex Kozinksi, "In Praise of Moot Court – Not!" (1997) 97:1 Colum L Rev 178 at 181.

11 See, e.g., the robust response offered by Michael V Hernandez to Alex Kozinksi's criticism of mooting: Michael V Hernandez, "In Defence of Moot Court: A Response to 'In Praise of Moot Court – Not!'" (1998) 17 Rev Litig 69; see also Dickerson, above note 2.

Canadian law schools strongly suggests that the argument in favour of moots is winning in the law student marketplace.

Conclusion

Moots (and other forms of law school litigation practice and other practice simulation exercises) are part of the Canadian law school culture. They may offer a form of "experiential" learning that law schools have been increasingly urged to include in greater measure in their JD programs. Moots also offer a uniquely intense and rewarding experience that many students greatly enjoy and that becomes for many among their most vivid and treasured law school memories.

Do moots help law students get jobs? Frankly, we don't know. But provided they do not occupy a disproportionate amount of a student's time or distract them from other enriching law school experiences, moots can be an exciting, "once in a law time" experience.

Appendix D: Moot Court and Other Law School Competitions [as of date of writing]

Competition	Area of Law/Type of Competition
Adam F Fanaki Competition Law Moot	Competition law
Arnup Cup Trial Advocacy Competition	Trial advocacy
Canadian Corporate/Securities Moot (sponsored by Davies, Ward, Phillips & Vineberg, LLP)	Corporate and securities law
Canadian Labour Arbitration Competition	Simulated labour arbitration
Donald GH Bowman National Tax Moot Court Competition	Tax
Gale Cup Moot	Canadian constitutional/criminal law
Harold G Fox Moot	Intellectual property law
Ian Fletcher International Insolvency Law Moot	International insolvency
Immigration, Refugee, and Citizenship Law Moot	Immigration, refugee, and citizenship law
Julius Alexander Isaac Moot	Areas of law involving issues of diversity and equity
Kawaskimhon National Aboriginal Law Moot	A non-adversarial negotiation on an Indigenous issue incorporating Indigenous legal orders and traditions alongside federal, provincial, and international law
Laskin Moot	A bilingual (French and English) moot dealing with administrative and constitutional law issues
Oxford International Intellectual Property Law Moot	International intellectual property law
Philip C Jessup International Moot	International law
Sopinka Cup	Trial advocacy competition
Walsh Family Law Moot	Family law
Warren K Winkler Class Actions Moot	Class action class certification hearing
Willem C Vis International Commercial Arbitration Moot	International commercial sales law and arbitration
Willms & Shier Environmental Law Moot	Environmental law
Wilson Moot	Legal issues concerning equality rights

part four
after graduation

10

after graduation from law school: bar, bay, and beyond

Introduction

Graduating from law school doesn't make you a lawyer. It's an important step, but it's just the first step. As a logician would say, a law degree is a *necessary* condition to becoming a lawyer, but it is not a *sufficient* condition. To become a lawyer after completing law school, you are going to have to take some additional exams and, in most cases, undergo some additional practical training. The exact details vary a little depending on which Canadian province you wish to become qualified to practise in and which law school you attended.

But not all law school graduates are interested in practising law – at least not as a lawyer in "private practice" at a traditional law firm. They may want to work as an "in house" lawyer at a company, a non-profit organization, a charity, or a non-governmental organization. They might wish to work for the federal government or for the government of a province, territory, or municipality. They may want to go into business, or even to teach law at a community college, high school, or law school. For that matter, they may wish to pursue a more creative and unconventional career path after law school, for example, as a writer, artist, or actor.

In a 2014 article by Janice Mucalov published by the Canadian Bar Association,[1] the author included a list of 48 "non-traditional" jobs for lawyers and an inventory of 43 different transferable skills that lawyers could bring to any number of different occupations.

Is it worth going to law school if you don't end up actually practising law? It might well be, especially if attending law school, directly or indirectly, expands your available career options. As one law school graduate who became a successful business executive once put it, "if you have a law degree, you can always go into business. But if you just have a business degree, you can't practise law."

But let's assume, for a moment, that you do want to practise law after you graduate, even if only for a limited time. What are the next steps after you have finished law school and are the proud holder of a JD degree? How do you become a lawyer?

---

1 Janice Mucalov, "Career Alternatives for Lawyers," Canadian Bar Association (September 1, 2014), online: https://www.cba.org/Publications-Resources/CBA-Practice-Link/Young-Lawyers/2014/Career-Alternatives-for-Lawyers.

What's in a Name?

Let's just digress for a moment to make sure we have the terminology straight. Lawyers are called many names – some of them are not very flattering, but leaving those sorts of names aside, there are many different technical names for lawyers used throughout the English-speaking world. Fans of American courtroom drama will be very familiar with the term "attorney." The word "attorney" as a synonym for lawyer (or at least one kind of lawyer) is common in the United States and some other jurisdictions around the world, but it is not used in Canada (except when referring to government prosecutors [Crown attorneys] and the principal government legal office [the Attorney-General]). The term "attorney" used to be widely used in Britain as a synonym for "solicitor," a term we will discuss below. This practice ended in 1875 with the passage in the UK of the *Supreme Court of Judicature Act, 1873*,[2] which, among other things, mandated that "attorneys," "solicitors," and "proctors"[3] would, from that point forward, all be called "Solicitors of the Supreme Court."

From 1873 onward, then, there were just two types of lawyers in the UK: barristers and solicitors. Barristers were traditionally the lawyers who argued cases in the superior courts. They were called "barristers" (a blend of "bar" and "ministers") because they were permitted to enter the courtroom area demarcated

2 36 & 37 Vict, c 66, s 87.

3 "Proctors" is an old term used to refer to people who had degrees in canon law from Oxford or Cambridge and received a licence from a bishop to practise in a kind of ecclesiastical court in the bishop's diocese called a "Consistory Court." See David M Walker, *The Oxford Companion to Law* (Oxford: Clarendon Press, 1980) at 1004.

by a rail, or bar. To be "called to the bar" meant that a person had satisfied the requirements imposed by the Inns of Court to argue cases. Solicitors, on the other hand, dealt directly with clients but performed lawyerly work that did not involve arguing matters in court. Wills and contracts, for example, were drafted by solicitors. But if a dispute arose over the interpretation of a will or a contract, barristers would be retained on behalf of the disputing parties (usually through an instructing solicitor) to argue the contested matter in the courts.

As we mentioned in chapter 4, the UK continues to have a divided legal profession today. A person who wants to become a lawyer can become either a barrister or a solicitor, but these alternative professional designations involve different routes to qualification, and you cannot simultaneously practise as both. In the Canadian common law provinces (that is, all provinces other than Quebec), the terms "barrister" and "solicitor" survive, but the Canadian legal profession is not a divided profession. That means that every qualified lawyer in each of the common law provinces becomes, by definition, both a barrister and a solicitor. The historical distinction between the two branches of the profession, however, is often retained symbolically, as you will see in a moment when we discuss the typical "call to the bar" ceremony.

Qualified Privilege

The process of becoming qualified to be called to the bar after you have graduated from law school is slightly different in each province. Let's take Ontario as an example. After graduating from law school, the next step is to register as a "licensing candidate" with the Law Society of Ontario, the organization that governs the legal profession in Ontario, and to register to write two long (4 ½ hours/160 items each), open-book, multiple-choice licensing examinations: the barrister examination and the solicitor examination. These examinations are offered three times a year, but as a practical matter most law school graduates choose to write them at the summer sitting in June right after they have graduated from law school. The Law Society of Ontario posts detailed information about the licensing examinations on its website.[4]

The next requirement that must be fulfilled in Ontario is completion of the "experiential training program" component of the licensing process. This requirement is satisfied by a lawyer-to-be in one of three ways:

- by completing an 8–10 month "articles of clerkship" (articling) with an experienced Ontario lawyer who has been approved by the Law Society of Ontario to act as a principal for this purpose;
- by completing the Law Practice Program (LPP), discussed below; or
- by having graduated from one of the two Ontario law schools that offer an integrated practice curriculum (IPC) that basically incorporates the experiential training component into the law school program itself. Those two law schools are the Lincoln Alexander School of Law at Toronto

4 Law Society of Ontario, "Guide to Licensing Examinations," online: https://lso.ca/becoming-licensed/lawyer-licensing-process/licensing-examinations/guide-to-licensing-examinations.

Metropolitan University and the Bora Laskin Faculty of Law at Lakehead University.

Articling

At one time, all prospective Ontario lawyers had to complete an articling requirement; there was no LPP or IPC alternative. This sort of legal apprenticeship gets its name from the document that the student and the supervising lawyer sign: the articles of clerkship. The word "articles" refers to the clauses of a contract or other legal document and, by extension, to the contract itself. So "articles of clerkship" meant a contract for a student to serve as a clerk under the supervision and tutelage of a practising lawyer. Serving as an articled clerk came to be known as "articling," and today it is more common for people to refer to law graduates at this apprenticeship stage of their careers as "articling students" rather than "articled clerks." The term "clerk" is now generally used to refer to law graduates who are completing their articles by working under the supervision of a judge or judges as a law clerk at a court, such as the Supreme Court of Canada, one of the provincial courts of appeal, or a federal or superior court judge.

The articling obligation is based on a traditional apprenticeship requirement for aspiring English solicitors. Fans of Gilbert and Sullivan may remember Sir Joseph Porter's Song from *HMS Pinafore* in which the pompous and most unseaworthy naval admiral explains the absurd story of how a successful legal and political career somehow qualified him to become a naval commander. One verse of the song refers to

Sir Joseph's "articling" experience and his subsequent qualification as a solicitor:

> In serving writs I made such a name
> That an articled clerk I soon became;
> I wore clean collars and a brand-new suit
> For the pass examination at the Institute[5]

The articling requirement has been a contentious issue for decades. An Ontario report as far back as 1972 recommended the abolition of the articling requirement. Critics note, moreover, that although the structure of law schools in the United States is similar to that of Canada, no similar lawyer apprenticeship requirement exists in 49 of the 50 US states. Even in the one state that retains an articling requirement (Delaware), it is far less onerous than the requirement of any Canadian province. Delaware requires applicants for bar admission to complete only a 12-week clerkship. More significantly, the 12 weeks need not be continuous, and they may be completed at any time after a person has begun law school. As a practical matter, then, any student who has worked as a summer associate at a law firm after their first and second year of law school will already have completed their clerkship requirement by the time they graduate from law school. Indeed, evidently, "almost all applicants accomplish the activities during one or more summers while they

5 William Schwenck Gilbert and Arthur Sullivan, *HMS Pinafore,* Act I, ll. 310–13, in Ian Bradley, ed, *The Annotated Gilbert and Sullivan* (Harmondsworth, UK: Penguin, 1982). The "Institute" refers to the Law Institution, the predecessor to the Law Society of England and Wales.

are in law school."[6] Can it reasonably be argued that Canada's lawyers are better trained and more qualified than lawyers at leading law firms in say, New York City, Chicago, or Los Angeles – none of whom has been required to complete articles of clerkship before being admitted to practice?

Articling has, however, generally enjoyed strong support among Canadian lawyers. In part, that support is based on a sincere belief that practical, law office training is an indispensable precondition of admission to the legal profession. As well, for at least some lawyers, articling is seen as a somewhat onerous but traditional rite of passage or orientation ritual that provides a unifying common ground of experience for members of the profession. Preservation of the articling system also offers some clear business advantages for some law firms. At smaller firms, articling students provide an important source of junior-level support that is very cost effective, not only because the salaries of articling students tend to be very modest – especially outside of larger urban centres – but also because the nature of the articling contract means that no commitment for any longer-term employment is assured, expected, or implied.

To be fair, though, the benefits to many small firms of employing articling students may often be outweighed by the costs – both in terms of compensation costs as well supervising lawyers' time. For some firms, then, agreeing to accept articling students represents a genuine financial sacrifice, undertaken in a spirit of selfless service to the profession and the public, not simply as a source of comparatively cheap labour.

---

6 Hon Randy J Holland, "The Delaware Clerkship Requirement: A Long-Standing Tradition" (2009) 78:4 Bar Examiner 28 at 29.

At the largest law firms, articling provides a unique opportunity to recruit new lawyers to the firm with what amounts to an unusually long probationary period of employment and at a salary level which, while comparatively high relative to entry-level positions in many other Canadian businesses, is much more modest than starting salaries of fully qualified lawyers.

Alternative "Experiential Training Programs"

Although articling continues to be a mandatory requirement in most Canadian provinces, in Ontario, since 2014, it has been possible for prospective lawyers to satisfy the necessary "experiential" requirement in alternative ways. This change to the Ontario lawyer qualification process came about as a response to an Ontario "articling crisis," which is briefly explained below.

Law Practice Program

The Law Practice Program (LPP) was introduced in Ontario in 2014. It was originally launched on a trial "pilot program" basis to offer law school graduates an alternative path to becoming qualified to practise law. Offering such an alternative path to qualification was a response to a significant gap in Ontario between the number of available articling positions and the number of law school graduates seeking to qualify for admission to the Ontario bar. This shortage of articling positions – particularly in the greater Toronto area (GTA) – came to be dubbed an "articling crisis."

There were several causes of this "crisis," including the increasing number of graduates of Canadian law schools, particularly Ontario law schools, where enrollments had increased by about 30 percent from 2000 to 2010,[7] as well as the growing number of foreign-trained applicants for admission to the bar, including a significant number of Canadian students who had chosen to study law at institutions outside Canada[8] with a view to returning home to practise. The shortage of articling positions – when completing articles of clerkship was a necessary requirement for anyone who wished to be called to the Ontario bar – was creating an insurmountable barrier to entry into the legal profession. Although some practising lawyers were wary of the swelling numbers of the profession, imposing such a barrier nevertheless seemed unfair and, in many cases, harsh and inequitable.

Having an alternative gateway to practice, then, which would be available to all seemed to represent a humane, sensible, and practical solution. But should the LPP be an *alternative* to articling, or should it replace articling altogether? Those who argued that the LPP should replace articling for everyone suggested that if the LPP were introduced only as an alternative

7 Malcolm Mercer, "The Never-Ending Debate: What Should Be Required in Order to Become a Lawyer?" *Slaw* (7 May 2018), online: https://www.slaw.ca/2018/05/07/the-never-ending-debate-what-should-be-required-in-order-to-become-a-lawyer/#_edn1.

8 A report for the Law Society of Ontario in 2016 stated that of the 2,350 new candidates to become licensed as lawyers in Ontario, about 600 were candidates who had received their legal education outside Canada, of which some 35 percent were Canadian-born candidates who had gone abroad for their legal education and were now returning to Canada to seek admission to the bar. See Law Society of Upper Canada, Professional Development and Competence Committee, "Report to Convocation" (22 September 2016) at 13, online (pdf): https://www.advocates.ca/Common/Uploaded%20files/Advocacy/Submissions/LawSocietyofUpperCanada/LSUC_PDC_Committee_Report.pdf.

way of satisfying a requirement for some practical training, there was a risk that a stigma might be attached to LPP students. It might be assumed that only those weaker students who had not been able to obtain an articling position would choose to complete the LPP, and that stigma might jeopardize their eventual employment prospects. Would it not be more fair and more sensible to replace articling with the LPP for all law graduates? In addition to preventing LPP alumni from being unfairly labelled, a universal LPP requirement might make it possible to ensure that all candidates for bar admission had practical experience of similar quality. It had long been recognized that individual articling experiences were vastly different and far from uniform in rigour and calibre.[9]

Defenders of the traditional articling system resisted such calls for a universal LPP requirement, and their voices prevailed. Articling therefore continues to be part of the legal practice environment in Ontario, although, with the LPP as an optional alternative, it is no longer necessarily part of every aspiring Ontario lawyer's experience.

The LPP consists of roughly 16 weeks of practice-oriented training in a "simulated work environment" followed by a four-month placement with a practising lawyer.[10] Most applicants

---

9 For an interesting assessment of articling, based in part on surveys of articling students and new lawyers, see the recent report released by the law societies of Alberta, British Columbia, Manitoba, and Saskatchewan, and the Nova Scotia Barristers Society: "Articling Program Assessment: Cross-Provincial Comparison" (25 April 2025) online at https://lawsociety.mb.ca/wp-content/uploads/2025/06/Articling-Program-Assessment-Cross-Provincial-Comparison-Report.pdf.

10 See, e.g., "Law Practice Program Training 2023 Portfolio," online: https://lpp.torontomu.ca/wp-content/uploads/2024/08/2023-24-TMU-Law-Practice-Program-Training-Program-Portfolio.pdf.

for admission to the bar in Ontario do still elect to satisfy the "experiential training program" requirement by articling. However, the LPP, as of 2022, boasted almost 2,000 alumni.[11]

Integrated Practice Curriculum

For a modest number of Ontario law school graduates who attended a law school with an approved integrated practice curriculum (IPC), it is not necessary either to article or to complete the LPP. Only two Ontario law schools, the Lincoln Alexander School of Law and the Bora Laskin School of Law, currently offer an approved IPC. An IPC, as the name suggests, integrates into the law school academic program itself the sort of experiential components that graduates of other Canadian law schools may only expect to encounter during articling or the LPP.

Why did the Law Society of Upper Canada (now called the Law Society of Ontario) approve only these two law schools to offer an IPC, the effect of which is to allow their graduates to avoid the need to article or to complete the LPP? The simplest answer is that no other law school in Ontario has sought such approval. If that seems surprising, one should recall again something that we have mentioned many times throughout this book: Law schools in Ontario are all university faculties, and for many law professors it is critical to the mission of university-affiliated law schools that they are not simply vocationally based "lawyers' schools."

11 Toronto Metropolitan University, "About the Law Practice Program," online: https://lpp.torontomu.ca/about.

But what about prospective law students? Might they not be so attracted by the chance to get a law degree that will concurrently satisfy the Law Society's "experiential training" requirement that the other six Ontario law schools that do not offer the IPC (University of Toronto, Osgoode Hall Law School of York University, Western University, Queen's University, University of Ottawa, and University of Windsor) would find themselves no longer able to compete for the best students? Although both the Bora Laskin School of Law and the Lincoln Alexander School of Law are relatively new, there does not, thus far, seem to be any indication that the six older Ontario law schools have struggled in vain to find strong students to fill their seats. There are undoubtedly advantages to both the traditional and the newer IPC approaches to legal education, and it may be supposed that each may appeal to a different segment of students.

It might also be noted that the opportunity afforded to graduates of one of the two law schools offering an IPC to skip articling may not have significant practical advantages for those students who wish to practise law at one of the larger firms in Toronto. It appears that, at least for the time being, these larger firms prefer to treat the graduates of all Ontario law schools alike – employing all of them explicitly as articling students (not lawyers) or, in some cases, using nominal distinctions but, for practical purposes, conferring upon graduates of IPC and non-IPC law school programs alike the same status as other articling students. Needless to say, this practice could evolve over time, and all Ontario law schools, likewise, may come to look very different in the years to come.

Articling in Other Canadian Provinces

The "articling crisis" was a uniquely Ontario phenomenon. In the other Canadian common law jurisdictions, an articling requirement remains a necessary element of the lawyer licensing procedure, although the required length of articling varies somewhat. In British Columbia, a nine-month articling period is required. In Alberta, the required period of articling is twelve months, but this requirement is reduced to nine months for students who complete the PREP course (discussed below) prior to articling. In Saskatchewan, Prince Edward Island, and Nova Scotia the required articling period is 12 months. In Manitoba, the required articling period is the "equivalent" of 52 full-time weeks, but this requirement may also be satisfied by part-time arrangements. In New Brunswick, the required articling period is 48 weeks. In Newfoundland and Labrador, a student must satisfy a 52-week articling requirement, but this includes six weeks spent in Newfoundland and Labrador Law Society's Bar Admission Course.

Naturally, it goes without saying that any of these requirements could be subject to further change in the future.

Bar Admission and Bar Preparation Programs

In Ontario, from 1959 until 2006, graduates seeking admission to the Ontario bar were required to complete a formal multi-month in-person "Bar Admission Course" run by the

Law Society of Upper Canada (as the Law Society of Ontario was then called).[12] The Bar Admission Course was offered at more than one venue in Ontario. However, by far the largest number of students attended the course in Toronto, which was taught at Osgoode Hall on Queen Street, the seat of the Law Society of Ontario as well as the location of the Ontario Court of Appeal and various court offices.

Ontario no longer offers a formal bar admission course. Students must self-study to prepare for the barristers and solicitors examinations. Many other common law provinces, however, continue to provide more formal bar preparation programs.

Four provinces, in fact, participate in a common bar preparation program: the Practice Readiness Preparation Program (PREP) created by the Canadian Centre for Professional Legal Education. Those provinces are Alberta, Saskatchewan, Manitoba, and Nova Scotia. British Columbia offers its own 10-week Professional Legal Training Course. The Law Societies of Prince Edward Island, Newfoundland and Labrador, and New Brunswick similarly offer their own bar admission courses, although we do note that New Brunswick has recently undertaken a Bar Admission Program

12 One of the authors of this book completed the original Bar Admission Course and, some years later, participated as a practitioner/instructor in the Bar Admission Course. We will leave it to astute readers to guess which author that was.

Development Project that may lead to changes to its bar admission program.[13]

The Call

For most law graduates, the culmination of their legal education comes when they are called to the bar and admitted to practise law. As we noted above, Canada has a unified profession: Every lawyer admitted to practise in any of the Canadian common law jurisdictions becomes both a barrister and a solicitor. Nevertheless, the traditional distinction between the two branches of the profession is formally observed in the ceremony by which students are admitted as practitioners. For example, when a person becomes a lawyer in Ontario, the ceremony involves two distinct elements: First, the Treasurer (or head) of the Law Society of Ontario convenes a Special Convocation of the Benchers of the Law Society and confers upon the candidates the degree of Barrister-at-Law and calls them to the Bar of Ontario (and thus makes them barristers). Then, convocation is adjourned and a special session of the Superior Court of Justice is immediately convened, presided over by a judge who administers the barristers and solicitors' oath,[14] and formally admits the candidates as solicitors of the Superior Court and Court of Appeal of Ontario.

---

13 See Law Society of New Brunswick, "Bar Admission Program Development Project," online: https://lawsociety-barreau.nb.ca/en/becoming-a-lawyer/bar-admission-program-development-project.

14 The text of the oath is found in Law Society of Ontario, By-Law 4, s 21(1).

Conclusion

The lawyer qualification process in Canadian common law provinces is long, arduous, and, frankly, expensive. To become a barrister and solicitor in Canada is, without doubt, an outstanding achievement, but it is important for anyone who is starting down the path to becoming a lawyer to be sure it is the right path for them.

part five
conclusion

closing statement

We've come to the end of our look into law school and the application process. So what are the key "takeaways"? Well, as a potential applicant myself with absolutely no background in the law, I am left with a lot to think about and digest. Here is a brief reminder of the topics we have tried to shed some light on through the previous 10 chapters.

To Apply or Not to Apply? That Is the ($315+) Question

Remember that applying to law school is expensive and gruelling. The admissions committee will look at your GPA and your LSAT score. They will also consider your extracurricular activities. Lastly, they will look at your personal essay. A personal essay is like an on-the-page interview. It is your one special shot to try to show the law schools what might set you apart, that you are more than your statistics, and how you could contribute to the law school and to the legal profession and broader community. Perhaps the most important takeaway from this chapter might be this: Given all the unknown elements that go into law school admissions decisions, there can be no guarantee that even very strong applicants will be admitted. But one thing can be said with certainty: There is only one way of having any chance of going to law school, and that is to apply.

The LSAT Laugh

If you want to apply to law school, the LSAT is a necessary evil. (Yup, not ideal for every candidate.) Logic, reading comprehension, and writing, oh my! The LSAT has changed many times since it was first launched in 1948 and, honestly, it could very well be different from the test we've discussed in this book by the time you read this. But the basic features of the test are likely to remain the same.

For better or worse, a high LSAT score is important for ordinary admission candidates. So, "write early and often" if necessary. Remember, no one cares how many times you take the LSAT. Schools will typically count only your highest score, or at least take account of the "progression" of your scores, and you are allowed to take it up to seven times in your life. Use them if you need them. The number of times you write the LSAT is between you and LSAC. (Well, between you, LSAC, and the admissions committee of every law school you apply to. But, to repeat, most schools are mainly concerned with your best score.)

Law School or Lawyers' School?

Let's face it. Many law graduates are still surprised about just how little law school teaches you about how to be a lawyer. This chapter tries to answer the timeless law students' question: why is this so? The answer lies in the unusual history of Canadian law schools, their unique role within the university, and the evolution they have undergone as they have imported traditions, particularly from the US and the UK. The chapter also canvassed the still current debate over whether law schools should have more practical, "experiential" aspects. Law school is a university faculty that opens the door to a professional field of practice. But the study of law is also the study of an important aspect of human civilization. Principles of law cannot be understood without a consideration of their practical impact. But practical skills alone do not reveal the richness and importance of law and legal traditions to human society. So the debate continues.

The Curriculum Basics

There is a National Requirement for common law school curricula in Canada, prescribed by the Federation of Law Societies of Canada. When you enter first year, most of your courses are going to be similar to the courses taken by your fellow first-year students at other Canadian common law schools. So, if you are lucky enough to be admitted, you will probably need to get ready for some courses in torts, contract law, property law, and criminal law.

The Socratic Method and Thinking Like a Lawyer

Dwight versus Langdell. Who was the better law professor? After a brief experience with the Socratic method myself while writing chapter 6, here is one piece of advice I might offer for future law students: It's a bit nerve wracking. Yes, I had the major advantage of being questioned by my father, not an imposing stranger, but it is still very intimidating being put on the spot. I thought knowing the facts of the case inside out would be enough. It's not. You have to understand the decision the judge made and the reasoning process the judge followed. You also need to form your own view on the fairness of the result and the soundness of the reasoning. And you need to be ready to back up your decision. I know my glimpse of the case method was pretty limited, but I must say I think I'm now a fan. I feel like I learned a lot about the case, and even felt I was working out how to decide it right along with the judge. Instead of just listening to a lecture and being told what the court decided, I felt completely submerged and involved. It honestly made learning about it fun. I must say, I didn't think I would ever say that about learning an obscure point about contract law from some old eighteenth-century auction dispute.

The Role of Statute Law: Interpretation Acts and Acts of Interpretation

This was my favourite chapter (if you were curious). It never really occurred to me how hard it could be to interpret a law. It almost makes me feel bad for mocking my Dad over the years every time he answered my questions with "it depends." Almost.

It still seems strange to me that there can be so much vagueness in our legal system. But I guess that is why the role of lawyers is so important and part of the reason lawyers need the sort of specialized education law school provides. This chapter was also an important reminder about what studying and practising law might really involve. If you find it frustrating or pointless to quibble over what a handful of words in an incomprehensible statute might or might not mean, you might want to think about turning around now. We are just scratching the surface of how detailed, picky, and tedious law can sometimes be. And as we've seen over and over throughout this book, law school isn't lawyer school. You are there to learn about the law. Not to practise what it's like to be Harvey Specter. Or Elle Woods.

The Dreaded Final Exam, The Bell Curve, Class Averages, and Why You Don't Need to Outrun the Bear

My immediate reaction to learning about mandatory law school class averages was probably the same as that of many first-year law students: It seems unfair that not everyone can get an A. After reviewing this chapter, though, my opinion has changed. It does make sense, to me anyway, to mark on the basis of a class average or a bell curve. And it does stop grade inflation if there is at least a rough limit placed on how many students in a class can get an A. It could also work in your favour. For example, suppose an exam is unusually hard and everyone in the class is at risk of failing. Not to worry. Suddenly a bare 50 percent might get you an A. It all depends on how you stack up compared to your classmates and, let's face it, the entire process of applying to law school will depend on how the admissions office judges your application compared to everyone else's. It is probably the fairest way, in my opinion, to grade law school students. Or the least unfair, anyway. And maybe that's the best outcome we can reasonably expect from any imperfect system.

Moot Courts and Mock Trials

What a moot point! Some professors love them. Some don't. The main takeaway from this chapter seems to be that moots can be a lot of fun and a good learning experience, too, but your regular school work should come first. It was also exciting to see how many opportunities are available to law students to compete in moots. And mooting might be your only chance to live out your dreams of being like Mike Ross.

After Graduation from Law School: Bar, Bay, and Beyond

The choice is yours. If you are lucky enough to get your JD, there will be a world of possibilities available. Do you write the bar? Article for a law firm? Or, in Ontario, do the LPP? Do you practise law? Do you use your degree for something else? It's really up to you. There is one thing for sure: You certainly haven't *closed* any doors by getting your JD.

Travels with My Father

I had the privilege of writing this book in many different places: from Stanford University in Palo Alto to Hawaii; from coffee shops in Oxford and Cambridge, England, to the sunshine of Spain and Portugal. Travelling while working on this book helped me remember that the world is a very big place with endless opportunities. There are a million different paths you can take and different careers you can pursue, with or without a law degree. Choosing to pursue a career in law should not be something you do because you feel like there is nothing else for you.

If you are also still on the fence about whether law school is for you, I hope this book will give you some insight into what you might be getting yourself into and help you, at least a little, make whatever decision seems best for you. And if in the end you decide you really are interested in pursuing a career in law, I sincerely hope this book helps you get there.

As for me, I have certainly enjoyed writing this book and learning so much more about law, law school, and the legal profession. I frankly still don't know, though, if law school is the right fit for me.

I suppose it just depends . . .

index

Page references in **bold** indicate a table.

about the authors

Victoria (Tori) Nicholls is a graduate of the University of Toronto (Victoria College). Since graduating, she has worked as a branch manager for a major retail business and as a professional services manager at a boutique law firm in Toronto. As a residence don at the University of Toronto, Tori saw how anxious many undergraduate students are to learn more about what is really involved in applying to and attending law school. An avid writer who has had a curious and sometimes critical bird's-eye view on the law for most of her life, she brings a fresh perspective to the hopes, fears, and uncertainties facing students who are wrestling with the question of whether applying to law school is the right decision for them.

Christopher C Nicholls is a professor of law at Western University's Faculty of Law where he is the inaugural holder of the W Geoff Beattie Chair in Corporate Law and a 2013 recipient of a Western University Faculty Scholar Award.

Professor Nicholls has been a Fulbright Scholar and Visiting Professor of Law at Harvard Law School, a Senior Visiting Research Scholar at Yale Law School, a Visiting Scholar at Stanford Law School, a Senior Visiting Academic at the University of Oxford Faculty of Law (HMC Commercial Law Centre), a Herbert Smith Visitor at the University of Cambridge, a Visiting Scholar at the University of Melbourne, and a Visiting Research Scholar at the University of Tokyo. In Canada, he was the inaugural holder of Dalhousie University Law School's Purdy Crawford Chair in Business Law and has also served as the Falconbridge Visiting Professor of Commercial Law at Osgoode Hall Law School and as a visiting professor at the law faculties of the University of Toronto and Queen's University. Prior to beginning his academic career, he practised corporate and securities law in Toronto and in Hamilton, Bermuda.

Currently a member of the editorial advisory board for the *Canadian Business Law Journal* (CBLJ), he previously served as the CBLJ's associate editor and corporate finance specialist editor, as a member of the editorial board of the *Canadian Journal of Law and Technology*, as research fellow with the Filene Research Institute (Madison, Wisconsin), and as head of research and policy at the Capital Markets Institute, Rotman School of Management, University of Toronto. In 2015, he was named a member of the Business Law Agenda Expert Panel appointed by the Government of Ontario's Ministry of Government and Consumer Services.

He is a past member (commissioner) of the Nova Scotia Securities Commission and, from 2016 to 2022, he served as chair of the board of directors of the Mutual Fund Dealers Association of Canada, one of two national financial industry self-regulatory organizations that amalgamated in 2023 to form the Canadian Investment Regulatory Organization (CIRO).

He has acted as a consultant to private law firms, government, and regulatory agencies and has lectured to academic and professional audiences in Canada, the United States, the United Kingdom, Australia, South America, and Japan.

He is the author of numerous articles in the fields of corporate law and governance and financial law and regulation, as well as seven other books on these and related subjects (two as co-author), including *Mergers, Acquisitions and Other Changes of Corporate Control*, 3rd ed (Toronto: Irwin, 2020), and *Securities Law*, 3rd ed (Toronto: Irwin, 2023).